P9-ELT-850

AMERICAN STRATEGY IN WORLD WAR II:
A Reconsideration

AMERICAN STRATEGY
IN WORLD WAR II:
A RECONSIDERATION

BY

KENT ROBERTS GREENFIELD

ROBERT E. KRIEGER PUBLISHING COMPANY
MALABAR, FLORIDA

Original Edition 1963
Reprint 1982

Printed and Published by
ROBERT E. KRIEGER PUBLISHING COMPANY, INC.
KRIEGER DRIVE
MALABAR, FL 32950

Copyright © 1963 by The Johns Hopkins Press
Reprinted by arrangement

All rights reserved. No part of this book may be reproduced in any form or by an electronic or mechanical means including information storage and retrieval systems without permission in writing from the publisher.

Printed in the United States of America

Library of Congress Cataloging in Publication Data

Greenfield, Kent Roberts, 1893-1967.
  American strategy in World War II.

  Reprint. Originally published: Baltimore: Johns Hopkins
University Press, c1963.
  Bibliography: p.
  Includes index.
  1. World War, 1939-1945—United States. 2. United States—
Military policy. 3. Strategy—History—20th century. I. Title.
[D769.2.G73 1982]   940.54′012   82-14881
ISBN 0-89874-557-8

10 9 8 7 6 5 4 3

To my colleagues
in military history,
1942–1958.

ACKNOWLEDGMENTS

THIS LITTLE VOLUME is based on the tenth series of J. P. Young Lectures in American history, which I had the honor of delivering at Memphis State University on October 28–30, 1962. The J. P. Young Lectureship is sponsored, and the lecturers appointed, by the University's Department of History, of which Professor Enoch L. Mitchell is Chairman. The lectures are made possible by the Herbert Herff Foundation.

My principal acknowledgments of indebtedness are to the historians who were my colleagues in the preparation of the U.S. Army in World War II, from 1946 to 1958, while I was Chief Historian of the Department of the Army. I am, in particular, indebted to Dr. Richard M. Leighton, who has given me invaluable criticism and made available to me unpublished information in the preparation of Chapters II and III; and to Professor William R. Emerson, who gave me the benefit of his suggestions and criticisms in revising Chapters III and IV. The whole text in its present form owes much to the critical reviews that Professor John L. Snell and Professor Louis Morton have given it. None of these scholarly friends is to be held responsible for my interpretations of the subject, but I owe a great deal to theirs, as the notes will indicate.

I am also gratefully indebted to Miss Elizabeth B. Drewry, Director of the Franklin D. Roosevelt Library at Hyde Park, and to her staff, for the search they made in the Roosevelt papers for notes in Mr. Roosevelt's hand that might throw additional light on his thinking.

The footnotes are not intended to indicate all the sources from which the information presented has been drawn. But I have introduced more than are usually included in a book not addressed to specialists. I have done this bearing in mind the probability that among the "general readers" for whom the book is primarily intended will be historians who, though not pursuing the subject as specialists, will have a legitimate professional interest in my sources of information, especially in regard to controversial questions.

The reader using the *Notes* and wishing to know the publication data regarding the works referred to can find this information through the index. Included therein are the short titles used in the notes (e.g. *AAF History;* Harrison, *Cross-Channel Attack*). The full title is in the first footnote referred to after the short title listed in the index.

The object of the lectures, here turned into a book, was synthesis and interpretation. The only information used that is based on the author's research in unpublished sources is reflected in the parts of Chapter IV that deal with the co-operation of air and ground forces.

KENT ROBERTS GREENFIELD

CONTENTS

AMERICAN STRATEGY IN WORLD WAR II:
A Reconsideration

INTRODUCTION

THE MAKING OF STRATEGY is a subject of intense public interest during the course of a war, not only because of its critical importance, but because, being an arcane operation, it offers a field for exciting speculation. When the facts about it eventually come to light it remains a fascinating subject if only because it represents a supreme effort of human will and intelligence to dominate the roaring flux of forces that are aroused by war.

The strategy of the coalition which defeated the Fascist Axis and Japan in World War II has an interest all its own because it produced, or (to speak more accurately) reflected and shaped, not only the most colossal but also the most devastatingly effective use of military force that history has yet recorded.

The essential facts about the strategic decisions of the Western Allies in that war are now known, at an extraordinarily early date after the war ended.[1] Never before have the veils of secrecy been removed as promptly and the record laid open to investigation. The facts are known. Interpretations of them differ, and will continue to differ as new generations approach these facts with new questions and with different prepossessions.

The studies in this volume would be open to serious criticism if they were intended to present a balanced story of American strategy in World War II. Their object, instead, is to present interpretations, reflections, corrections, and questions. Undoubtedly they will be found to raise more questions than, in the present state of knowledge, one can answer.

One object of the present review of interpretations is to bring to public attention and discussion points of view that have been expressed, some quite recently, by scholars who have studied intensively the wealth of information now available and have tried to strike a balance between conflicting judgments based on that information.

I have focused these studies on grand strategy, that is, on strategy at the highest level of outlook and decision. This book will, therefore, deal only incidentally with campaign or field strategy, or even with the use that commanders of the great theaters of operations, such as Eisenhower, Nimitz, or MacArthur, made of the forces allotted to them, though that is a highly important subject in the history of the war as the United States waged it. Furthermore, the present discussion, which is centered on the strategy of "our side," of the powers allied against the tripartite Axis, is focused on the evolution of an American grand strategy. If for no other reason this is necessary because the picture of British strategy is still incomplete, and even more so is that of our dark and massive wartime ally, the U.S.S.R.

I

ELEMENTS OF
COALITION STRATEGY

A REMINDER OF SOME of the major strategic decisions of the Allies in World War II seems appropriate since the momentous events of our days are already crowding the memory of that war from the minds even of those who lived through it as adults, not to mention readers for whom it is only history. The decisions here selected for recall have not been chosen as representing a consensus of informed historians as to which decisions were the most critical or important. They are recalled only to set the stage for what is to follow.

One of the foundations on which American strategy was built had already hardened into a national resolution before the United States entered the war. This was that the national interest of the United States required the survival of Great Britain and its postwar freedom of action as a great power. It was embodied in the policy of the President to which the nation gradually rallied in the interval between the fall of France in June, 1940, and December 7, 1941.[1] It remained the foundation of American strategy throughout World War II.

Eight Strategic Decisions

First: the decision that the overriding aim of the coalition would be the complete defeat of its enemies. The three principal members would not stop fighting until they had these enemies at their mercy. This meant, to use the terms now current, that they resolved to wage unlimited, or "total" war. This decision was never in debate. From first to last it was the goal of Great Britain and the Soviet Union, which were striking back at an enemy that had ruthlessly hit and cruelly devastated both of them. As far as we, the Americans, were concerned, it was implicit in our planning and preparations for war even in 1939–41 when our declared national policy was still the defense of the Western Hemisphere.[2] Meeting with the British in December, 1941, in the ARCADIA Conference, as soon as we were at war, we declared that the total defeat of Germany and Japan was our aim as well as theirs. Practically speaking, this amounted to aiming at unconditional surrender. Much tension and debate has since arisen regarding the wisdom of having declared unconditional surrender to be our war aim, but during the war it was never vigorously opposed or even seriously debated as a guiding principle of our strategy. The Allies came to terms with Badoglio's rump government of Italy while Mussolini, though overthrown, was still not securely in their grip, but this they did in order to concentrate more effectively on crushing the spider at the center of the Axis web. They allowed Japan to retain a symbolic emperor, but only when they had the Japanese at their mercy. Total victory, a common aim reflecting a profound determination, was pursued without serious compromise until its grim consummation had been achieved in 1945.

Second: the decision of the United States that Germany was the Number One enemy. This meant that the coalition would direct its main effort against Germany until the German government surrendered unconditionally. With the British and the Russians, both fighting angrily for survival, this view of the right strategy was a foregone conclusion. Acceptance of it by the United States meant that the Americans might have to be content with containment and harassment of the Japanese, the enemy that had hurt them, until the defeat of Germany was assured. The decision of the Americans to identify themselves with it is therefore remarkable. The American military authorities did so a year before the United States got into the war.[3] They saw it as the only strategy that was consistent with assuring the survival of Britain.

Third: the decision of Britain and the United States in July, 1942, to invade North Africa.[4] This decision, carried out on November 8, concentrated in the Mediterranean the bulk of the forces available to the Western Allies in Europe, until the spring of 1944. It led to the conquest of the North African shore of the Mediterranean from Morocco to Egypt; the surrender of 275,000 Axis troops in Tunisia in May, 1943; the conquest of Sicily two months later; the overthrow of Mussolini; the surrender of the Italian government in September, 1943, and a campaign in Italy that continued until the liberation of that country in May, 1945. With the conquest of Sicily the Western Allies achieved air supremacy in the Mediterranean and reopened the Mediterranean as a thoroughfare for their shipping. Invading the mainland of Italy they promptly secured bases for a two-way bombing of Germany. In the winter and spring of 1942–43, as the Allies drove from east and west in Africa toward victory in Tunisia, and the Soviet armies counter-attacked from the ruins of Stalingrad, the Allied coalition had begun to gain, and the Axis to lose, the strategic initiative in the European war.

Fourth: the decision of the Western Allies to give a combined bomber offensive directed at the vitals of the German nation a major claim on their common resources in 1943. This decision was reached when Churchill and Roosevelt, and the Combined Chiefs of Staff, met at Casablanca in January to decide on the courses of action to be followed in 1943. American participation in this combined bomber offensive did not, in 1943, produce the effect that enthusiasts for air war had predicted. But the commitment to it, and the effect that it seemed likely to achieve in 1943 were among the major factors that determined the limitation of American combat ground strength to eighty-nine divisions.[5] It had much to do with the fact that the American Army that emerged to fight the decisive battles of 1944 had a long-reaching, heavy, and powerful air fist, and a comparatively small though compact ground fist. This in turn reacted on the ultimate strategy of the coalition. In the spring of 1945, though in victorious pursuit of the Germans, the Americans could not deploy enough ground combat strength in Europe to adopt without grave risk Mr. Churchill's proposals for resolute opposition to the oncoming Russians, even had Mr. Roosevelt been convinced of the wisdom of taking an open stand against them. In Asia, if we had had more divisions to deploy in 1944–45, we might not have felt it necessary to invoke the active support of Russian arms to pin down the Japanese army in Manchuria. For the same reason we lacked the means, during those years, to contain or effectively oppose Mao Tse-tung's Communists in China.

Fifth: the decision of the American Joint Chiefs of Staff to take swift advantage of the great victory of the U.S. Navy at Midway in June, 1942, by allowing Admiral Nimitz in the Pacific Ocean Areas, and General MacArthur in the Southwest Pacific, to engage in limited offensives.[6] This was the first step in the departure of the Americans from the basic Anglo-American strategic agreement, dating from early 1941 and ratified at the ARCADIA Conference, that the strategy of the Allies would be only to contain Japan until they had made sure of the defeat of Germany. By February, 1943, Admiral Nimitz's commanders had wrested Guadalcanal, and General MacArthur's the eastern tip of New Guinea, from the Japanese. The Americans went over to the offensive and began to gain the initiative in the Pacific, the secondary theater of warfare, as soon as they did in the war with the Axis in Europe, the primary theater. Also, as a consequence of the American decision in July, 1942, to engage in limited offensives against Japan, and the dim prospect of a cross-Channel attack before 1944, the Army had more troops, ground and air, deployed against Japan at the end of 1942 than in the European theaters of war.[7]

Sixth: the decision approved at the first Quebec Conference in August, 1943, less than a year after the attack on Guadalcanal, to let Admiral Nimitz launch an amphibious offensive through the Central Pacific in 1944, simultaneously with General MacArthur's drive toward the Philippines in the Southwest Pacific.[8] This meant that in 1944 two powerful offensives were racing toward the same goal, the Luzon-Formosa-China Coast triangle. By October, 1944, while the Allies were still battering at the Siegfried Line in Europe, both of these offensives reached the Philippine Sea; and that of Admiral Nimitz, through the Central Pacific, had brought the B-29 superbombers of the Army Air Forces within bombing distance of Tokyo.

Seventh: a decision on the importance of which no emphasis is needed: the agreement of the Allies on a power-drive of combined arms across the English Channel, aimed at the heart of Germany.[9] This, and the massive offensives of the Soviet armies met in the heart of Germany in April, 1945. The strategic pattern for the defeat of Germany was set at the Tehran-Cairo, or SEXTANT-EUREKA, Conferences of the three Allies in November–December, 1943, when the decision on a powerful cross-Channel attack was after long debate made firm and final.

In contrast, a strategic pattern for the defeat of Japan was not finally determined until the decision to drop the atomic bomb was made—in the last minute of the war. In the war with Japan the force of events exerted an influence not as accurately foreseen as in the war with Germany, and had more to do with the outcome than any single formal decision on strategy—such as that of the Western Allies to stake the outcome in Europe on a power-drive across the Channel. The final pattern would depend on the effect of the naval blockade, the outcome of the two American offensives racing across the Pacific, and of the strategic bombing of the Japanese homeland. That much of the design was set by the end of 1943. It included Soviet entry into the war against Japan, and the defeat of Japan eighteen months after the surrender of Germany.[10]

The decision chosen as Number Eight remained an integral part of this evolving plan until the atomic bomb was dropped. It seems a paradoxical choice for it was a decision never carried out.

Eighth: the decision that an invasion of the Japanese homeland, as well as blockade and bombing, would have to be built into the strategy of the Allies to insure the defeat of Japan. This decision is important for its political as well as for its military consequences. It led the Western Allies, especially the United States, to encourage the Soviet Union to enter the war against Japan, and it affected the decision to use the atomic bomb.[11]

Not included in the foregoing list is the decision announced at Casablanca in January, 1943, that unconditional surrender was the war aim of the Western Allies. It is omitted because its sudden announcement by President Roosevelt was primarily a political move. I have not found any conclusive argument or evidence regarding its military effect. As an aspect of strategy it was, as already intimated, part and parcel of the determination of the Allies to make a complete defeat of the Axis and Japan their paramount war aim. The only question that remains is whether it was expedient for Mr. Roosevelt to proclaim it when he did in the terms of his unconditional surrender formula, and stick to that formula as stubbornly as he did.

Basic Principles

This brings us back to the decision at the top of the list: the resolution of the Allies to make the total defeat of their enemies the aim of their strategy. This was the declared aim of all three in Europe, and of the Americans and the British in their war on Japan. It meant, as already observed, that they intended to wage unlimited war; and they did. The military leaders of the United States, though not Mr. Roosevelt, had made this the basis of their strategic calculations before we entered the war and while we were still trying our best to keep out of it. As soon as we got into the war, Mr. Roosevelt adopted their plans.[12] We acted on the principle: "There is no alternative to victory."

It was a daring commitment. In December, 1941, Britain and Russia were fighting with their backs to the wall and the United States had come in half prepared, with its only serious ready weapon reduced to smoking wreckage in Hawaii and the Philippines. Britain and the United States immediately formed an interlocking directorate, pooled their resources, placed all of these that they could spare at the disposal of the embattled Russians, and began at once to concert plans for a world-wide offensive on the assumption that they could bring to pass the utter defeat of both the Axis and Japan, even if Russia went under before they achieved it. In an effort to characterize the strategy of World War II nothing seems more fundamental than the resolution with which the Western Allies adopted this aim, the consistency with which the coalition adhered to it, and the foresight and thoroughness with which the Allies planned, developed and applied their resources, economic and military, with this goal kept steadily in mind.

Much could be said, and has been said, about this underlying determination and basic determinant of Allied strategy in World War II. It had an effect that was fateful for the Japanese. Their Government had carefully planned a limited war with the United States.[13] Counting on our unpreparedness and our anxieties about Europe, and on the fact that the fangs of Germany were in Russia's throat, the Japanese believed they could gain objectives that would assure their supremacy in China and Southeast Asia, and that we would come to terms with a *fait accompli*. They might well have succeeded if we had met them on their own terms. They counted on our acceptance of limited war in the Pacific. Our initial strategic decision that, until the defeat of Germany was assured, we would fight only a war of containment in the Pacific seemed to mean that their assumption had been correct. But surprisingly soon they ran head on into our determination not to play out the game of war on those terms. As soon as the battles of the Coral Sea and Midway in May and June of 1942 gave us a chance, we began to carry out a strategy that was aimed at their utter defeat. This is why I mentioned the decision of July 2, 1942, to launch limited offensives in New Guinea and Guadalcanal. By September, 1943, when we were closing in on their fortress air-and-naval base at Rabaul, and had decided to unleash Admiral Nimitz's drive through the Central Pacific, they saw that we had the means as well as the determination to destroy them as a military power. They realized too late, as Admiral Yamamoto sadly admitted, in a much misinterpreted remark, that if we chose to wage unlimited war, they could gain their objectives only by invading the United States and dictating their terms in the White House.

As for the defeat of Germany, the key to the strategy of the Western Allies was their decision to put their main weight into a cross-Channel invasion of France, aimed at the heart of Germany—the decision for OVERLORD. It became final with the appointment of General Eisenhower as Supreme Allied Commander in December, 1943. It was reached after the longest and most anxious strategic debate of the war—between the British and the Americans—one that is renewed with each new book on strategy, in spite of the fact that the attack was so triumphantly successful. The debate is intensely interesting because in it all the strategic issues of the war were weighed by the protagonists, each in his own scale of values.

The fact in that debate most important in a characterization of Anglo-American strategy is that they did not make their decision to launch a cross-Channel attack final until both of the Western Allies were convinced that it made military sense.[14]

The proposal was made by the Americans in April, 1942, for reasons rooted in three necessities of the situation as they saw it: the strong pull of the Pacific war, which threatened to dissipate their then limited resources; their need of a plan that would concentrate these resources where they could be effectively delivered; and their desire to get Germany knocked out at the earliest possible date. In April,

1942, therefore, they proposed that the Allies immediately start building up their strength in England to launch a cross-Channel attack in the spring of 1943 (ROUNDUP), meanwhile preparing to launch a minor attack (SLEDGEHAMMER) in the fall of 1942, if necessary. They justified their daring plan by invoking the classic "principles of war": concentration of force; the offensive; attack from a secure base at the end of America's shortest line of supply. The British, eager to have American strength committed in Europe and concentrated in England at once, agreed in principle. But they quickly decided that the American plan of immediate attack (SLEDGEHAMMER) was impracticable, and even reckless, and began to condition their agreement, then withdrew it. In July, Mr. Roosevelt intervened and overruling his military advisers supported the British proposal that the Allies use their ready forces to invade North Africa. This killed the possibility of ROUNDUP in 1943.

Once the Allied forces in Europe were concentrated in the Mediterranean it made military sense to use them there as long as they could not be used elsewhere, and they were used to reopen the Mediterranean and knock Italy out of the war. The Americans had to be satisfied with the combined bomber offensive as the only means available in 1943 for a direct body blow at the Germans. For them the Mediterranean was an indecisive theater, and with increasing anxiety and impatience they pressed the British for a commitment to a full-bodied attack across the Channel in the spring of 1944, and finally, with a welcome assist from Stalin at Tehran, they got it.

The Americans believed that the British were contending

for a strategy that was unsound in principle and suspected that they were swayed by political interests. The British regarded the Americans as doctrinaire and "rigid" in their strategic thinking. Actually, after the decision for TORCH, which was Mr. Roosevelt's, there was no serious disagreement among the Allied military chiefs over what, in general, had to be done next, nor was there a real disagreement on fundamentals.[15] Both sides agreed that Germany was the Number One enemy. They were in full agreement on continuous and violent offensive action. Both agreed that a final knockout thrust would be necessary and that this should be directed from England through France. They were in agreement that this should not be undertaken until Germany had been weakened by encirclement, air bombing, and Soviet onslaughts; or, to use the language of the bull ring, until the strength of the bull had been sapped by the picadors and banderillos. The basic question was not a question of principle but the question of how soon a concentrated blow should be delivered, and what degree of concentration was essential.

In short, the Western Allies decided to make OVERLORD their main effort in Europe only when they agreed that such an effort made military sense. Considerations other than purely military affected the positions taken by Mr. Churchill, Mr. Roosevelt, and the military chiefs on both sides, in the course of the debate, and help to account for the tenacity with which they stuck to their positions. But in every case these positions were finally rejected or accepted on the ground of military expediency. The same statement can be made about the other strategic decisions mentioned above. A political element, not to mention other nonmilitary elements, can be found in all of them. But this was submerged. Political considerations affected the debates, but had a minor effect on their outcome. All but one of the eight decisions were based on an agreement by the Anglo-American military chiefs that the decision represented, in each case, the most effective use the Allies could at the moment make of their military resources to achieve their common end, the utter defeat of Germany and Japan.

The exception is TORCH, the decision to invade North Africa. In this case Mr. Roosevelt overruled the military judgment of his Chiefs of Staff and his Secretary of War, directing them to use our forces in the invasion of North Africa, which Mr. Churchill and the British Chiefs wanted, and the American Joint Chiefs had strongly opposed. The British may have acted on political rather than military motives; many Americans, including our military chiefs, thought so. As for Mr. Roosevelt, he justified his decision by affirming his desire, as war leader of the American nation, to have American ground forces engage in large-scale offensive action in Europe in 1942. But if he was animated by nonmilitary considerations, he had made a move that was highly politic in a military sense if only because it broke a dangerous Anglo-American deadlock over strategy. It also conformed to the military principle of utilizing ready forces at the first opportunity to pass to the offensive, if you can thereby inflict serious damage on the enemy. It certainly did not mean that Mr. Roosevelt had decided to put America's military might at the service of the British in regaining their empire.

Military versus Political Considerations

The common strategy adopted by the three principal Allies advanced their political interests in different degrees. Mr. Churchill was repeatedly disappointed that the strategy agreed on was not in better accord with what he regarded as the political interests of the British Commonwealth and Empire, and toward the end, with what he conceived, and as it would now seem rightly conceived, to be the common political interests of the Western democracies vis-à-vis the Soviet threat. Mr. Roosevelt decided that the interests of the United States would best be served by letting the judgment of his military advisers prevail, and these invariably closed ranks in favor of decisions that could be justified by military ends as against those that could not. Stalin knew what he wanted in concrete terms, and he got it. But he gained the political advantages he wanted without infidelity to military commitments on his part, which his Allies fully agreed to be necessary. The Western Allies acted on the assumption that their political interests would best be served by subordinating them to the one aim on which, from first to last, they were completely agreed: the total military defeat of their enemies. Wise or unwise, there is nothing surprising about this. It reflects a tendency inherent in coalition strategy. Among powerful Allies as disparate in their political interests as the United States, Great Britain, and the Soviet Union it can be defended as having been the height of political wisdom.

In the first period of the coalition when its members

were off balance and still had reason to doubt whether they could achieve their audacious war aim, a strategy that did not subordinate everything to military considerations would have been risky indeed. By mid-1944 it was clear that they had the means to achieve their primary aim in fairly short order. Even then the question of letting their military decisions deviate from a strictly military line did not until the very end produce any serious disagreement between the Western Allies.

Much has been made of the political wisdom of Mr. Churchill's yearning to go into the Balkans.[16] That yearning Mr. Roosevelt spiked by pointing out that the Balkans were an area where American public opinion would not let him use American forces. More plausible was Mr. Churchill's eagerness to have an Allied force, supported by Tito's irregulars, slice through Istria and the Ljubljana Gap to Vienna. Such a move might well have put our troops in Vienna ahead of the Russians.[17] But in November, 1944, the Russians themselves seem to have been undecided as to whether they might not prefer to have the Allies press forward with their plans for Italy and the Mediterranean, which if successful would have put them in a position for a drive toward Vienna, rather than insist on having them open a "Second Front" in northern France.[18] At Tehran, Stalin came out strongly for the cross-Channel invasion. But a year later he was suggesting an Allied drive from Istria toward Vienna "to assist in the advance of the Red Army through Hungary." [19]

The question whether the Western Allies should let political considerations sway them in the joint use of their forces became serious very late in the war. It arose only when the Soviet armies surged into Poland and the other states that lay between the U.S.S.R. and their rendezvous with the Allies in the heart of Germany. Stalin was giving more and more grounds for suspicion that, without departing from the strategy on which all agreed, he was using the military power this gave him to convert these states, once and for all, into Communist satellites. Mr. Herbert Feis has gone over this whole ground with great sobriety and thoroughness in his book *Churchill, Roosevelt, and Stalin*. Though as convinced as any of us that Stalin was a shrewd and unscrupulous ruffian, he has shown how hard it was for the Allied leaders, including Mr. Churchill, to convince themselves of this at the time. But Mr. Churchill presently began to sound the alarm, and to sound it with increasing urgency, in Allied counsels, above all with his "great friend" Mr. Roosevelt. He first tried to get Mr. Roosevelt into a working agreement among themselves and with Stalin on politico-military spheres of influence in liberated Europe. Mr. Roosevelt declined.[20] He acted on the assumption that the Soviet Union could take what it wanted in Eastern and Central Europe whether we consented or not. He could not be persuaded that what we could hope to get from Stalin only by threats of military non-co-operation justified risking the military estrangement of Russia. A purely military strategy again prevailed.

Finally, during April and May, 1945, Mr. Churchill, now desperately concerned, urged that the Anglo-American-French armies be rushed forward in Germany to meet the Russians, and be withdrawn into the prearranged zones of occupation only when Stalin relaxed his grip on Eastern and Central Europe. Mr. Truman, then President, believed that to do this would sacrifice a last chance to get the U.S.S.R. to take its place in the United Nations; and for the Americans the effective organization of the United Nations was the most important political aim of the Allies.[21]

In the last phase of the war, when the coalition was no longer bound together by the iron strap of danger, when the question was no longer whether, but how soon, it would win; the period, therefore, when it seemed safer for its members to maneuver for postwar political positions, the United States threw its whole weight against deviation of the Western Allies from a military strategy until victory was complete. By this time Mr. Roosevelt had become unhappily aware of what Stalin was doing, and so was his successor in the presidency, Mr. Truman. But both stuck to the policy of resisting, to the limit of their power, making political commitments to either of their Allies until victory had been achieved, and the Americans were now wielding a power that the British could no longer successfully oppose. Both presidents consistently gave the green light to their military chiefs, and these consistently rejected decisions on grounds other than military effect. General Marshall, surely one of the most statesmanlike of them, wrote to General Eisenhower when Mr. Churchill, in late April, 1945, was urging the political advantages to be gained by liberating Prague, and as much of Czechoslovakia as possible, before the Russians arrived on the scene: "Personally and aside from all logistical, tactical or strategical implications I would be loath to hazard American lives for purely political purposes." [22]

Neither the military chiefs, then, nor the two presidents

were unaware of the political risks they were taking; but they were alike convinced that the political temper and interest of the United States required that they thrash the bullies that had disturbed the peace, and get American soldiers and sailors home.[23] This conviction was so deeply ingrained in American traditions and habits of thought that it cannot reasonably be argued that any other policy would have been politically feasible. Mr. Roosevelt and Mr. Truman had to convince themselves, and apparently did, that this policy of political disengagement and their political objective—an effective organization of the United Nations—could be reconciled.

The American view prevailed because in the period of the war at which we have arrived, the United States had achieved a massive preponderance of weight in the Western Alliance. British mobilization, production, and military capacity reached their peak in 1943. By the following spring, at the time of the cro..s-Channel invasion, there was a rough parity between the deployed forces of Great Britain and the United States. From then on the military contribution of the British levelled off or declined, while that of the United States continued to increase. By 1945 the military weight that the United States could throw into the scales of strategic decision was decisive.[24]

The decision to invade Japan illustrates the vast repercussions that a decision made within the terms of reference just outlined could have. American military planning for the defeat of Japan included from its inception in 1943 preparations for an invasion of the Japanese home islands with forces to be redeployed from

Europe after the defeat of Germany. The planners hoped that the Soviet Union could be induced to take some of the weight off of the American effort by striking at the Japanese forces on the Chinese mainland, and when in October, 1943, and again at the Tehran summit conference in November, Stalin gave his word to do so, they were relieved and happy. In 1944, with OVERLORD launched and prospering, the American Joint Chiefs, now better prepared to calculate the forces they would have available to deploy in the Pacific after the surrender of Germany, devoted their attention to devising a strategy designed to finish off Japan. Convinced that invasion would be unavoidable and that it would be a long and bloody operation, they attached great importance to the collaboration of Stalin.

Before the end of 1944, the outlook in the Pacific brightened. We had got within bombing distance of Tokyo; the Navy had disabled the Japanese fleet and cut off all of Japan's lines of supply; and MacArthur was going ashore in the Philippines ahead of schedule. But our strategists were still unable to convince themselves that they could avoid an invasion that would be fearfully costly in American lives. When therefore at Yalta, in February, 1945, Stalin reaffirmed his promise, and made it specific as to date and plans, the American military chiefs welcomed the pledge. But at Yalta Stalin also stated his price in political terms, to be paid by China. This was a disturbing departure from the principle which the three Allies had followed in Europe that political commitments would be postponed until the unconditional surrender of the Axis had been achieved. Mr. Roosevelt, accepting the judgment of his military advisers, underwrote the payment of Stalin's price.

Soon thereafter it became evident that Stalin, overriding the protests of his Allies, was bent on consolidating his political position in advance of victory in Europe as well as in the East. The American presidents, in deciding whether to yield to the increasingly anxious pleadings of Mr. Churchill and take a firm stand against Stalin, not only had to weigh the risk to which they would expose the success of the United Nations, they had also to weigh the advice of their Army chiefs and commanders, including General MacArthur, that Russian intervention was needed to mitigate the terrible cost of invasion against the opposition of the Japanese fanatically defending their homeland.[25] In the spring of 1945 Stalin's exactions everywhere had become so manifest and formidable, and the prospects of breaking Japan by blockade and bombing so bright, that Admiral Leahy and Admiral King, within the Joint Chiefs of Staff, fell away from the view that Soviet aid was needed. But the view of General Marshall and the Army prevailed that invasion would be necessary, and that it could be effective, without an intolerable cost in American lives, only with Soviet help; and the President, in dealing with Churchill and Stalin, acted on the advice of the Joint Chiefs of Staff to that effect. Again, a strategy based squarely on military considerations prevailed.

The foregoing discussion is not intended to present a well-rounded picture of Allied strategy in World War II. Not included, for example, is the strategy of the Allies in China-Burma-India, though it most strikingly illustrates the complications and frustrations that could be, and in this case were, injected into the strategy of the Allies by the divergent political interests of Great Britain and the United States, intensified by American aims incommensurate with the forces committed to their achievement. But the strategic decisions in the principal theaters of the war lend strong support to certain general propositions regarding the remarkably effective strategy of the Western Allies which a historian is now justified in making.

The most striking is that in the decisions by which Anglo-American strategy was directed, military considerations consistently prevailed. They prevailed in the clinches of debate because, given the aim of inflicting total defeat on a powerful combination of enemies, strictly military considerations seemed, and probably were, the only ground on which a coalition with disparate political interests could be held together until that ambitious aim was achieved. It seems further clear that the American determination to concentrate on military victory, combined with the increasing military weight of the United States in the Western Alliance, was responsible for causing this view to prevail.

A second observation can be made which is the obverse and corollary of the first. This is that, if in the determination of Allied strategy political considerations exercised only a negative influence, that is why, if for no other reason, the strategic direction of World War II by the Allies is a classic model of military effectiveness in achieving the arduous aim that the architects of their strategy set for themselves.

II

AMERICAN AND BRITISH STRATEGY: HOW MUCH DID THEY DIFFER?

IT IS GENERALLY AGREED that the Anglo-American coalition in World War II was the closest and most effective partnership in war that two great powers have ever achieved. Their strategy evolved in an unbroken series of agreements as to what it was necessary or desirable io do next in order to gain a maximum of military advantage from the situations that successively confronted them. But these agreements were attended by controversy. This revolved around the cross-Channel attack of the Allies. Flaring up first within six months after the United States entered the war it continued until the invasion of France was well on its way to success in August 1944. The controversy generated a heat that at times seemed to endanger the Anglo-American alliance, and it has continued to generate heat in the histories and memoirs of the war.

Dr. Richard M. Leighton has recently recalled attention to this controversy in studies based on his research in the logistics and strategy for the United States Army's history of World War II.[1] He has concluded that the suppositions that animated it, particularly those of the Americans, were unfounded, and that the British were on firmer ground in suspecting the motives and intentions of the Americans than the Americans were in suspecting those of the British.

In short, he has challenged the version of the controversy that has become all but a stereotype in American thought about Allied strategy in the war.

According to this version the heated debates between the Americans and the British that preceded their decisions arose from opposing conceptions of strategy. The Americans believed in concentration of power at the earliest possible moment at a decisive point, and the delivery of a blow to the solar plexus. The British believed that the correct strategy was to work vigorously but more cautiously from a ring which sea-power and Russia's resistance enabled the Allies to close around Axis-dominated Europe; keep the Russians supplied and fighting; blast and burn the German and Italian cities with bombs; stir up and arm resistance in the occupied countries; jab through the ring whenever an opportunity presented itself, while ever tightening it, until the enemy was so strangled and bled that the final offensive need be only a coup de grâce.

American writers on the subject have consistently represented OVERLORD—the great cross-Channel drive launched in June, 1944—as a triumph of American over British views. They have maintained that the British, though they repeatedly accepted a decisive power-drive in principle, did everything they could to evade or postpone its execution; that Mr. Churchill having induced Mr. Roosevelt to put the bulk of our forces into the Mediterranean in November, 1942, the British became intent on keeping them there indefinitely; and that only by dint of persistent argument and pressure the Americans, with decisive support from Stalin at Tehran, finally succeeded in getting Allied strategy back on the right track. The result, after some further displays of reluctance, was British support for a cross-Channel drive to the heart of Germany, and a spectacular success. This is commonly represented, in American writings, as a triumph of the American conception of correct strategy imposed on the unwilling British.

Dr. Leighton sharply challenges the view that the British tried to evade a cross-Channel invasion in 1944, and gave their support to it only under pressure from the Americans. He finds no evidence for such evasiveness except in the suspicions of the Americans. His conclusion is that the successive agreements that defined the course of Anglo-American strategy were governed by practical considerations, of which, in 1942–43, the most pressing was the availability of critical military resources. To these practical exigencies both Allies had to trim their concepts, interests, and desires. In the end the course they pursued conformed more closely to the British concept of sound strategy than to that for which, after March, 1942, the Americans persistently contended.

Basic Principles and a Proposed Speed-up

Dr. Leighton reminds us that as soon as Pearl Harbor brought the United States into the war the two Allies agreed, in principle, on the strategy by which they would be guided. They reached this agreement at the so-called ARCADIA conference, which, immediately after Pearl Harbor, brought Mr. Churchill and Mr. Roosevelt, and the British and American Chiefs of Staff together in Washington. The strategy agreed on was as follows:

1. Beat Germany first, meanwhile containing the Japanese.

2. Wear down the strength of the enemy by closing around Axis-held territory a ring to be tightened as fast as the resources of the Allies permitted.

3. The means to be used: naval blockade; all-out aid to the Russians; strategic bombing; intensive cultivation of resistance in Nazi-occupied countries; limited offensives with mobile forces at points where locally superior Allied forces, particularly forces strong in armor, could be brought to bear with telling effect—all directed toward a final knockout punch.

No plan for a drive to the heart of German power then seemed possible to envisage and none was developed.

But only three months later the Americans proposed such a plan which, if adopted, would be a radical departure from the ARCADIA agreement. They proposed that the Allies proceed at once to the blow that would knock Germany out of the war. Dubbed BOLERO-ROUNDUP, it called for concentration in the United Kingdom of all the then available resources of the Allies (BOLERO). This was to begin at once and be given first claim on all new resources as they became available, with a view to launching a massive power-drive across the English Channel in the spring of 1943 (ROUNDUP). Forty-eight divisions would be used— over 1,000,000 Americans in thirty divisions, the rest British. The Americans would also supply a powerful air force to be combined with British air in support of the operation. The assault would go in on a six-division front, between Le Havre and Boulogne, with 77,000 men, 18,000 vehicles, and 2,250 tanks.[2]

To this master plan the Americans attached a rider, known as SLEDGEHAMMER. This was to prepare an assault force to be launched across the Channel in September, 1942. By then only three and a half American divisions could be made available in England, and only enough landing craft to put the combat elements of two divisions ashore in the assault.[3] SLEDGEHAMMER was to be undertaken in only one of two contingencies: (1) if the Russians were on the verge of collapse, in order to create a diversion that might keep them from capitulating; or (2) in the unlikely event that the Germans were crumbling and a small-scale invasion might suffice to finish them off.

The BOLERO-ROUNDUP plan originated in the War Plans Division of the War Department General Staff, to which it offered the solution for a problem that seemed all but desperate. The United States, thrown on the defensive at Pearl Harbor, unready for war in spite of its preliminary mobilization, saw its unfinished structure of forces and materiel now being dismantled and dribbled away in small packets to meet demands for reinforcement from all over the world. Nobody could see an end to this dissipation. On December 15, General Marshall had brought young Colonel Eisenhower into his War Plans Division and in February made him its Chief. In January Eisenhower wrote in his notes to himself: "The struggle to secure the adoption by all concerned of a common concept of strategy is wearing me down. Everybody is too much engaged with small

things of his own. We've got to go to Europe and fight—
and we've got to quit wasting resources all over the
world." [4]

Into this chaos General Eisenhower's Division projected
its plan for a cross-Channel drive through France into
Germany, in 1943. It was so beautifully logical, so completely an expression of the principles of war and it also
answered so perfectly the need of the Americans to stop
the scatteration of their strength and get it mobilized to
end the war in Europe at the earliest possible date, that
the War Department, including the ambitious young American air force, fell in love with it, and the Navy accepted it.
F.D.R. approved it and in April sent General Marshall and
Harry Hopkins to London to sell it to the British.

To the relief and jubilation of the Americans the British
accepted it. Eisenhower now wrote in his notes: ". . . at
long last . . . we are all committed to one concept of
fighting! [Now] . . . we won't be just thrashing around
in the dark." The Americans at once put BOLERO—the
build-up in the United Kingdom—into effect. But the
British soon began to express anxiety about SLEDGEHAM-
MER, and finally concluded that that would be a rash and
unfeasible undertaking. SLEDGEHAMMER was a subordinate
feature of the American concept and the Americans could
not press hard for it since the British would have to provide most of the force necessary for its execution. But the
Americans refused to abandon it. When in June the American and British Chiefs came to a deadlock over SLEDGE-
HAMMER, the American Joint Chiefs went to Mr. Roosevelt
and proposed that the United States suspend its support of
the whole BOLERO-ROUNDUP plan and go all out against

Japan in the Pacific. The President firmly said, "no": that would be a little like threatening to "take up your dishes and go home," [5] and in July he sent Harry Hopkins, General Marshall, and Admiral King to London under firm orders to agree with the British on some plan that would bring American ground forces into action in Europe before the end of the year.

The result was TORCH and the invasion of North Africa in November 1942.

Encirclement Pursued: the Mediterranean and Pacific Offensives

The American military chiefs were bitterly disappointed by the decision for TORCH. Eisenhower said on the day of the decision that he thought it "could well go down as the 'blackest day in history'." [6] It threw the Americans' carefully arrayed plans into confusion. They saw all their disposable strength, including the troops, equipment, aircraft, and assault shipping that had already been built up in the United Kingdom under BOLERO, being sucked into the Mediterranean. Concluding that TORCH would make ROUNDUP in 1943 an impossibility, the Army chiefs were again left with no master plan to govern the mobilization of their military and productive resources. To the American military chiefs TORCH meant that Allied strategy had been diverted from the highroad to victory into a dead-end theater from which no decisive blow at Germany could ever be delivered.

When Churchill, Roosevelt, and the Combined Chiefs of

Staff met at Casablanca in January to decide what they could do in 1943, both sides readily agreed that their three primary tasks for the year were to quell the U-boat menace, get all possible aid to Russia, and concentrate their air power on the bombing of Germany. The sore point was what to do in the Mediterranean. The declared objective of TORCH had been to occupy North Africa and reopen the line of communication through the Mediterranean to the Middle and Far East. But Mr. Churchill and Mr. Roosevelt were now talking cheerfully about using the forces victorious in Africa for an invasion of Sicily, not only to complete the security of this line, but as a step toward knocking Italy out of the war. This, said Mr. Churchill, with unfortunate rhetorical exuberance, would be "to strike into the underbelly of the Axis."

The Americans, having no alternative to offer, accepted the invasion of Sicily. It clearly made military sense to keep the only Anglo-American forces that were in contact with the Germans fully employed in wearing them down as long as any object of strategic importance was within reach. But in the vista that now seemed to be opening, the American military staff and chiefs anxiously foresaw a progressive commitment to the Mediterranean of ground strength and amphibious lift which would make it possible for the British to argue successfully against a cross-Channel attack even in 1944. For at Casablanca their conviction hardened that the British would hold out for a peripheral strategy—what one irritated American officer called "periphery pecking." Secretary Stimson later called it "pinprick warfare." [7] The suspicion had already taken root that when the British argued for a "flexible" strategy, as against an overriding commitment to ROUNDUP in 1944, they were also intent on securing their imperial interests in the Mediterranean.

Suspicion had become conviction in the stern, unbending mind of the American Navy's Chief, Admiral Ernest J. King. He had backed the BOLERO-ROUNDUP plan vigorously only in order to get the war in Europe out of the way quickly. He now, in the spring of 1943, easily won from his American colleagues authorization to "extend" as well as "maintain" "unremitting pressure on the Japanese." [8] This was a departure from the basic agreement of the Allies on the conduct of the war. It seemed to the British that the Americans were saying to them: "if you insist on committing our strength in Europe to indecisive employment in a theater in which your interests are paramount, we will insist on reserving a larger share of our growing resources for the theater in which our interest is paramount."

The American Army staff went home from Casablanca convinced that they had been outwitted and outmaneuvered by the British. General Wedemeyer, General Marshall's chief adviser at that conference, wrote: ". . . we lost our shirts . . . we came, we listened, and we were conquered." [9] They determined never to let it happen again. Beginning with the next conference with the British in May (the TRIDENT Conference) they went to these "summit" meetings with the British—QUADRANT at Quebec in August and the Cairo-Tehran conferences in November and December—armed to anticipate and counter every imaginable argument of the British and backed by ranks of experts whose brief cases bulged with studies and statistics; and they devoted themselves to getting Mr. Roosevelt to throw his weight in their favor. They concentrated their growing argumentative skill and resourcefulness on getting from the British an inescapable commitment to a cross-Channel invasion in force in the spring of 1944.

A 1944 Cross-Channel Attack Desirable: Is it Feasible?

At each of the conferences the British readily agreed to accept a cross-Channel drive in the spring of 1944 as a major Allied objective.[10] But they refused to commit themselves to a conclusively dated decision until conditions could be foreseen that would give the operation a reasonable chance of success at that date; and they argued earnestly that the only correct strategy was to remain flexible, that is, free to adopt alternative moves until the last possible moment. To the Americans such flexibility seemed irreconcilable with the complex business of organizing, assembling, and mounting a huge expeditionary force and providing in time the equipment to meet its multifarious specialized needs. And the conditions which the British attached to ratification of their consent deepened the suspicion of the Americans that the British meant to evade or postpone indefinitely a direct blow at Germany through France, and were wedded to a peripheral strategy and an inconclusive opportunism. Anxious over what they believed —with some justice—to be Mr. Churchill's proclivity, they even feared that the British would try to involve them in an invasion of the Balkans. To their great relief Stalin, at Tehran, threw his weight on their side, and insisted on giving OVERLORD (as it was now called), and a complementary invasion of southern France (ANVIL), first claim on all the resources of the Allies. The British offered no objection to this. Eisenhower was chosen to be Supreme Commander. The point of no return had been passed.[11]

Even so, and even after OVERLORD was launched, the Americans, still suspicious of the uses the British wished to make of American forces in the Mediterranean, pressed hard for the invasion of southern France, which was repeatedly postponed until it finally went ashore on August 15. By then the Americans had beaten down the last claim of the British on the American divisions required for a strong push into northern Italy. Indeed, it was in this hassle that the Anglo-American conflict of interest over the Mediterranean entered its most acrimonious phase, and the Americans for the first time rode rough-shod over the unanimous military judgment of Mr. Churchill and his military chiefs, leaving them feeling, as Mr. Churchill wished Washington to know, "that we have been ill-treated and are furious." [12]

Dr. Leighton, in the study mentioned above, argues plausibly that if in 1943 the British were reluctant to sacrifice all other projects in Europe to a cross-Channel attack in 1944, they had as much ground for suspecting the Americans' real intentions as the Americans had for suspecting theirs. This becomes clearer if one looks more closely at the question of nuts and bolts, or, to speak more grandly, at the logistics of strategy. For the *sine qua non* of a strong assault on the coast of France for which the Americans were contending was enough assault landing craft, which only the Americans were in a position to supply.

At the TRIDENT Conference in May the question of assault shipping—above all of tank-landing ships (LST's) —came into focus as the critical factor in planning for a 1944 cross-Channel assault. The American Joint Chiefs brought to the conference a plan for a massive cross-Channel blow in the spring of 1944 on much the same scale as their plan for ROUNDUP in 1943. The British experts immediately challenged and demolished the Americans' assumption that enough landing craft of the needed types would be available to carry out the heavy assault that they proposed. It had to be recognized that without more assault landing craft, particularly without more LST's, the best that the Allies could hope to achieve in the spring of 1944 was an initial assault by only three divisions, backed by two afloat, against the armed and defended coast of France. It was assumed, and was reasonable to assume, that not as large an assault force would be needed in 1944 as in 1943, since it now looked as if the combined bomber offensive would have knocked the *Luftwaffe* out of the air over France by May, 1944. But a five-division assault against "Fortress Europe" would have less initial punch and be smaller by almost half than the eight-division assault that the Allies were about to launch against the lightly defended coast of Sicily in July, 1943. Facing up to the facts, the Combined Chiefs agreed to plan for a cross-Channel assault of this modest weight, plus two airborne divisions. In all twenty-nine divisions, including those to be assembled in the United Kingdom ready to be fed into the lodgment area, were to form the Allied invading force.[13]

Obviously, to have any chance of success an assault on this scale would have to be attended by very favorable conditions. One was Allied supremacy in the air. Another was that only a limited number of German divisions should be in France to oppose the invasion. This being so, the British urged their contention that to keep German divisions away from France the Allies should press the Germans harder in the Mediterranean where they then had them on the run. The Americans continued to argue that this violated the principle of concentration at the decisive point. They at least obtained a joint declaration that all future operations in the Mediterranean should be planned to prepare the way for the cross-Channel invasion.[14]

A Dilemma: How Find Enough Assault Craft?

It had become sharply clear at TRIDENT that the critical item limiting the prospect of a cross-Channel attack in 1944 was tank-landing-ships (the LST). This put the Americans in an awkward bind. The LST was a British invention, but in 1943 only the Americans were equipped to produce LST's or other large landing craft in anything like the necessary quantity and, unlike small landing craft, LST's could be built only in shipyards capable of producing large vessels for the Navy. Furthermore the American chiefs had agreed that the building of LST's was an American responsibility. But they had fully committed the qualified shipyards to the production of other types of ships. The first charge on Navy shipyard capacity had been the construction of escort carriers and destroyer escorts to quell the submarine menace. This was agreed to be right and proper when the Combined Chiefs at Casablanca in January had made anti-submarine warfare the first charge on all the resources of the Allies. The peak of this load on the shipyards had passed in March. But crowding it for priority was the stupendous task of constructing a new, modernized United States fleet to replace the one shattered at Pearl Harbor, and equip the Navy to drive the Japanese out of the Pacific.[15] And when the turn of the LST's came, Admiral King would certainly claim the bulk of them to carry out the operations in the Pacific which he and Admiral Nimitz were now planning, under the authorization that he had obtained at TRIDENT, to expand the Navy's offensives against the Japanese.

The British were well aware of all this. And it put them in a position to think (and to say): "If we are to have a power-drive across the Channel in 1944, on whose prior claim to our joint strength you are so insistent, only you Americans can provide the means indispensable to its success." [16]

Meanwhile, the Combined Chiefs had taken a practical step which was more important than anyone could then foresee. This was to create a small headquarters under General Sir Frederick Morgan, who was designated COSSAC —that is, Chief of Staff to the [future] Supreme Allied Commander.[17] At TRIDENT, giving General Morgan the strength of assault there agreed on as predictable, they instructed him to work out, within its limits, a plan of attack for a cross-Channel invasion on May 1, 1944 and estimate the conditions necessary for its success. He would then submit it for judgment as to whether the Allies could safely adopt it.

To this complex, laborious, and baffling task General Morgan and his staff applied themselves with remarkable breadth of vision and integrity of purpose. From the first, General Morgan instructed his staff not to think or act as planners but as the embryo of the future Supreme Headquarters. He had his plan ready to submit when the Allies met again at Quebec in August. There the Allied chiefs— Mr. Roosevelt, Mr. Churchill, and the Combined Chiefs— adopted it, and they now authorized General Morgan, subject to their approval, to issue the necessary orders for the assemblage of forces and the preparatory operations that his plan required.

OVERLORD (as it was now called) had passed from planning to preparations keyed to an accepted plan. But nobody was happy about its prospects. Its execution remained highly conditional. And the conditions turned, and continued to turn, on the limited strength allotted to it at TRIDENT, a five-division seaborne assault, supported by two airborne divisions. The Allies had committed themselves to its execution as their main objective in Europe. But by putting a ceiling on the size and strength of the force to be used they had got themselves into the position of giving their chief operation for 1944 a strictly limited claim on their resources, while their other enterprises became the residuary legatees of American production, which was now beginning to pour out munitions and supplies in an abundance beyond expectation.

The British, and the United States Army staff, were dissatisfied with the modest scale of invasion adopted. Mr. Churchill asked for a twenty-five percent increase in its strength. But no action was taken. It did not make sense to build up a more massive attacking force without a reasonable hope of having in hand enough assault craft to lift it. Assault shipping, above all the LST, remained the crux of the problem, and the key to its solution was in the hands of the Americans, and specifically, barring intervention by the President, in the hands of Admiral King.

A month after Quebec the Navy ordered the construction of landing craft.[18] In October the American shipyards began to launch LST's at the rate of about twenty a month. But Admiral King laid claim to all but three months of this output as necessary for the great amphibious drive through the Central Pacific which the Combined Chiefs had authorized him to launch, and Mr. Roosevelt made no visible move to deny his claim. Only the November, December, and January output of LST's was allocated to OVERLORD.[19] General Morgan soon pointed out that the new LST's promised, plus the LST's to be transferred from the Mediterranean, would still not be enough even for the mimimal OVERLORD required by his plan. On November 5, Admiral King offered a bonus of twenty-one LST's from his allocation—hardly "a princely gift," Dr. Leighton remarks, since it was to be made up from production that exceeded his original calculations of his requirements and since not all of the additional craft he offered could arrive in time for a May 1 OVERLORD. That operation —now less than six months away—was still left with a big deficit of assault ships. If OVERLORD was to be executed, it was clear that the deficit would have to be made up either at the expense of the Pacific in which the American interest was paramount, or of the Mediterranean in which the British interest was paramount. Such was the situation on the eve of the "showdown" Cairo-Tehran conferences in November and December, 1943. The British had served notice that they would demand a review of the relation between the Mediterranean and OVERLORD. The Americans, therefore, went to the conference tense and anxious about the positions that the British would take, and feeling that only a firm stand by Roosevelt and Stalin could save OVERLORD.

The proposals of the British proved to be anything but unreasonable, and after meeting with Stalin at Tehran, the Allies came back to Cairo committed to an agreement that a May, 1944 OVERLORD was to have first claim on the resources and military efforts of the Allies, world-wide. This was what the Americans had been contending for since TRIDENT. But to the British it might well seem a concession, since for the first time it put into reserve for that operation the assault shipping in the Pacific, which Admiral King, firm in his skepticism about British intentions had guarded as sacrosanct and not even to be discussed with the British.[20]

Still to come was a hassle over means with which to carry out operations in the Mediterranean during the winter and spring that the Cairo-Tehran agreements recognized as desirable. As soon as Eisenhower and Montgomery got into their OVERLORD saddles in January, they demanded that the assault on Normandy be greatly strengthened—which created a big new demand for landing craft. How meet this and at the same time find enough to put three divisions ashore in an invasion of southern France (Operation

ANVIL), which the Americans insisted on mounting simultaneously with OVERLORD? In Italy the amphibious end-run to Anzio in January failed dismally. "I had hoped," said Mr. Churchill, "that we were hurling a wild cat onto the shore but all we got was a stranded whale." The Anzio beachhead had now to be defended and reinforced. Finding enough LST's and other landing craft to meet all these requirements tested to the limit the ingenuity and tempers of both the English and the Americans. But by "veering and hauling," trimming and recalculating, and by the postponement of ANVIL, the assault shipping for a much expanded OVERLORD was found, and the biggest amphibious force in history, which had been given the objective of driving to the heart of Germany, was lifted across the Channel on June 6.[21] No one doubts that the British put everything they had into the final strain and effort that made this possible.

British Contributions and Reasons for Caution

Looking back one can now see that from the first the British had taken an impressive number of practical measures that paved the way to success for the invasion of France. If they refused SLEDGEHAMMER, they did not flinch from undertaking alone the bloody cross-Channel raid on Dieppe as early as August, 1942. It was a failure. But the British diligently wrung from the experience lessons that were valuable in making OVERLORD successful.[22] It was the British who invented and first engineered the instrument of war, the LST, that made a cross-Channel assault in force a feasible military operation. It was Mr. Churchill who dreamed up, and the bold ingenuity of his engineers that constructed, the indispensable offshore harbors by which the Allied expeditionary force was supplied over the beaches throughout the summer and fall of 1944. General Morgan (COSSAC) was a British officer, completely loyal to the concept of a cross-Channel invasion. He had an able American deputy and an Anglo-American staff. But from first to last COSSAC got more vigorous co-operation and support from the British than from us. It was COSSAC that brought planning down out of the clouds into the realm of problem-solving, and this, in my opinion, had more effect than any other one thing in bringing to pass a firm agreement to see OVERLORD through. British urgings in 1942 took us into the Mediterranean where in the spring of 1943 the Anglo-Americans bled the Axis in Africa. The Allies then invaded Sicily, thereby shaking down Mussolini's regime and bringing about the surrender of Badoglio's Italy. Thereupon, staging a major campaign on the mainland, they pinned down and wore out the divisions Hitler threw into Italy after Badoglio's surrender, and by arming and supplying Tito's guerillas kept wastefully occupied the German divisions with which he garrisoned the Balkans. These measures were taken in compliance with British arguments. In these arguments the British may have been—and probably were—animated by their own political interests, but the arguments made military sense. From QUADRANT on it was Mr. Churchill and his military chiefs, and not the Americans, who urged the need for a stronger cross-Channel assault, and certainly they pulled their full weight in the provision of ocean shipping and

other measures to insure a build-up for the invasion that
would make it decisive. As early as May, 1943, they had
activated an army group and an army headquarters that
went to work on detailed plans for the assault, in contrast
with the Americans, who made no similar provision until
October.[23] In short, it can be plausibly argued that it was
the British (and Mr. Roosevelt) who are to be credited
with the realistic approach to OVERLORD that insured its
success.

The effective co-operation of the British and Americans
in World War II was an unprecedented achievement in the
history of nation-states. But the fact of mutual suspicion
remains, standing out more starkly against the lack of any
evidence, except the suspicion of the Americans, that the
British were ever unfaithful to their repeated pledge to
support a full-bodied cross-Channel attack—always with
the proviso that the situation as the due date approached
must be such as to offer a reasonable prospect of success—
a proviso that certainly made common sense.

It cannot be denied that the British approached ROUNDUP
and OVERLORD more cautiously than the Americans, and
this is not surprising in view of past experience and their
situation in 1943.

In 1942 they were suffering from fresh and terrible
wounds that made them more feelingly aware of German
might than we could be. The insistence of the American
military chiefs on SLEDGEHAMMER, in the spring of 1942,
had undoubtedly confirmed their impression that the Americans were as reckless as they were inexperienced in military affairs. A year later General Marshall admitted that
SLEDGEHAMMER might have been suicidal.[24] The British,

although they acquired a genuine admiration for Marshall and Eisenhower, could not overlook the fact that neither of them had ever commanded even a regiment in battle. They were naturally convinced of the superiority of their own military wisdom based on experience and were disposed to regard the Americans as bright but annoyingly persistent children. Nor could they dismiss the grim memories of their experience in World War I. Then, when for once they had committed a huge ground force on the continent, they had seen a whole generation of young Englishmen destroyed. Churchill's mind was haunted by the thought of the Channel running "red with the blood of British and American youth" and the beaches "choked with their bodies." [25] When the Americans pointed to the overpowering resources they could put behind a cross-Channel drive, the British remembered the similar promises we had made in World War I and then had failed to make good, except in manpower. This time we more than made good. We delivered, by 1944, an overwhelming abundance of materiel, on time, at the decisive points. But in 1943 what the British had before them was the fact that the Americans were offering to put in the Channel by 1 May 1944 only enough LST's for an attack that would be anything but overwhelming.

As the hour for OVERLORD drew near, the British had a very grave reason for caution as they counted what it would cost them in basic strength as a world power. They were facing the fact that in the fall of 1943 their economy and military manpower were mobilized to the limit of endurance. They had far more to lose than the Americans.

OVERLORD on a big scale would be their last shot. Even if it succeeded, they would be unable to replace the losses it would inflict. The strength of their nation would decline not only relatively to that of the United States, but absolutely, leaving Great Britain a second or third-rate power in world affairs. Failure of the invasion would mean, if not ruin, a prolongation of the war all but certainly beyond their power to sustain. These prospects they weighed with deliberation in the fall of 1943 and accepted with characteristic realism and courage as they made their final commitment to OVERLORD.[26]

Was American Strategy Excessively Rigid?

The British, on their part, did less than justice to the Americans in blaming them for rigidity in their military thinking. "The President," exclaims Mr. Churchill in his memoirs, "was oppressed by the prejudices of his military advisers," and lets us know in a well-known outburst of impatience how oppressed he himself felt by the "American clear-cut, logical, large-scale, mass-production style of thought." [27] The English seem not fully to have grasped either the capabilities or the limiting conditions of the American system of industrial production. When the American military chiefs insisted on adoption of a plan with a target date long in advance of a large operation, it was because they could not see how otherwise in a huge mass-production economy such as ours, they could ready for a great offensive, forces armed with intricate mechanized equipment whose production had to be scheduled back through the whole war economy, and whose delivery and supply on the far shore required the preparation and assembly of a fleet of ships of all kinds; not to mention the task of keeping all these requirements co-ordinated with the demands of the other theaters of a world-wide war. Given our highly subdivided system of mass-producing the complex and varied implements of modern warfare, it can be argued that the American military chiefs, far from being rigid theorists, were guided by practical sense in insisting on steadfast adherence to large and definitely scheduled objectives. As Gordon Harrison has observed, when Mr. Churchill characterizes our undeviating adherence to a cross-Channel attack on a given date in the spring of 1944, as typical of American mass-production thinking, this amounts to accusing the Americans of having a mass-production economy.[28] The corollary of the British concept was elasticity, the seizure of opportunities as they arose, the shifting of forces from one point to another, to take advantage of the enemy's weakness. The experience of TORCH should have been enough to show that this was no easy matter once a large force was committed and its massive structure of overseas bases and communications established. This was a fact that Mr. Churchill's restless imagination seems never to have grasped.

Finally, it must be said in justice to the Americans that when Mr. Roosevelt gave the English so much anxiety by loosening the tether on Admiral King and General MacArthur in the Pacific, he was favoring the evolution of a strategy more appropriate to a global two-front war than rigid adherence to the Germany-first strategy.

The Resolution of Differences

In their debates about the cross-Channel attack and Mediterranean operations the British and Americans both argued tenaciously for their points of view and their vigorous, and sometimes heated, debates left a mark on their strategy. But they always ended with a compromise agreement on what to do next. Two forces, I believe, kept them together. One was the determination of Mr. Roosevelt and Mr. Churchill that everything else must be secondary to the solidarity of the Anglo-American alliance. The other was common sense, or preferably perhaps, a capacity to deal sensibly with concrete issues as they arose, on which both the Americans and the English pride themselves as a quality in their common tradition of jurisprudence and management of affairs. Thanks to their determination to stick together and to move only by steps on which they could agree, the strategy they actually pursued reflected the concepts of both. Step by step throughout 1943, they moved nearer to concentration on the massive blow that the Americans desired, but this step-by-step advance permitted much of the elasticity and follow-up of immediate opportunities in which the British believed. In the plan that was executed each side got in fair measure what it had contended for. The ring around the area controlled by the enemy had been tightened until it was becoming a noose. His cities had been blasted and burned, his air force knocked out of the sky over France. The resistance in Jugoslavia and France had been armed and organized. "His armies had been dispersed, pinned down and bled by concentric Russian and Allied offensives until he could no longer form an effective reserve for counterattack. To this extent the strategy urged by the British had prevailed, with tremendous effect." If the Americans had had their way and ROUNDUP had been launched in 1943, it would have been a one-shot affair which, if it had miscarried, could have been disastrous. At best it would not improbably have led to the slaughters that the British dreaded. On the other hand when OVERLORD came, "it was the power-play for which the Americans had always contended, and the Allies put behind it the force and weight needed to drive it to the heart of Germany." [29]

Looking back now, it is interesting to observe that the strategy in Europe which the Americans followed, step by step, as events unfolded, and which they found it wise to follow, was much closer to that which the British proposed at the ARCADIA Conference in December, 1941, and which the Americans had then accepted, than it was to the deviation from that strategy which the Americans proposed in the spring of 1942, and for which for more than a year they vociferously contended.

III

FRANKLIN D. ROOSEVELT:
COMMANDER-IN-CHIEF

No QUESTION HAS ARISEN regarding the extent to which President Roosevelt exercised his powers, personal and official, as war leader of the American nation between 1939 and 1945. For better or for worse, he dominated the scene. This is a fact that was then, and is now recognized by his friends and enemies, admirers and detractors, and is not likely to be questioned by future historians.

The subject under consideration in what follows is not this, but the question of his influence on the military conduct of the war as waged by the United States. This resolves itself into the use he made of his authority, under the Constitution, as Commander-in-Chief of the armed forces. This authority of the American president is undefined and it has never been possible to distinguish it sharply from his other powers. But the theme of the present chapter can be exactly defined. It is Mr. Roosevelt's exercise of that power in decisions that, whatever their motivation, had a marked effect in determining to what uses the military resources of the nation were put.

Conflicting Impressions

On Mr. Roosevelt's use of his military authority a variety of views has been expressed.

Robert Sherwood set the stage for the commonly accepted view in his authoritative and invaluable *Roosevelt and Hopkins*, in 1948, when he said that there were "not more than two occasions in the entire war when he [Mr. Roosevelt] overruled his Chiefs of Staff." [1]

John Ehrman, the judicious and perceptive author of two volumes on *Grand Strategy* in the British official history of the war, takes the view implied in Sherwood's statement. General Marshall, he writes, "more than any one man conceived the American strategy," and he accepts Mr. Stimson's valedictory conclusion in 1945: "His [Marshall's] views guided Mr. Roosevelt throughout." [2] In the U.S. Army's history of the cross-Channel attack Gordon Harrison wrote: "He tended to make only the large decisions as between fully developed alternative courses of action . . . The President generally appeared at the Allied conferences as the defender of the strategy worked out by the Joint Chiefs of Staff." [3] The authors of the Army's volumes on strategic planning Maurice Matloff and Edwin Snell, have taken a like view. Field Marshal the Viscount Alanbrooke, Chief of the Imperial General Staff, has left no doubt of his conclusion. "The President," he wrote in an "after-thought" in his diary entry for June 26, 1942, "had no great military knowledge and was aware of the fact and consequently relied on Marshall and listened to Marshall's advice. Marshall never seemed to have any difficulties in controlling any wildish plans which the President might put forward." [4]

But now hear Admiral Leahy, Chairman of the Joint Chiefs of Staff and the President's own Chief of Staff, who saw him, he says, almost every day. "Planning of major campaigns was always done in close co-operation with the President. Frequently we [the Joint Chiefs] had sessions in his study." And again: "Churchill and Roosevelt really ran the war . . . we were just artisans, building patterns of strategy from the rough blueprints handed us by our respective Commanders-in-Chief." [5]

In a recent study of the war powers of the American President, Professor William R. Emerson, maintaining that Mr. Roosevelt's influence on the course taken by American strategy in World War II has been obscured by his characteristic indirectness, concludes that he not only followed his own ideas about strategy, but "did not hesitate to ignore or override" his military advisers in deciding by what means these ideas should be carried out. [6]

In the observations about Mr. Roosevelt cited the term "strategy" has a variety of meanings. If by strategy one means the conception of grand objectives and "blueprints" of plans to achieve them, then the view of Mr. Roosevelt's role taken by the Army's historians quoted above can hardly be contested, and Admiral Leahy's statement is misleading. But the aspect of strategy of primary concern to the historian is the end result, the course of action finally adopted and followed and its military consequences. In this view of strategy the relative importance of Mr. Roosevelt's influence stands out in high relief.

Without going beyond the published histories one can

count more than twenty cases in which Mr. Roosevelt over-ruled the considered judgment of his responsible military chiefs and substituted for theirs his own estimate of the military situation, or his own concept of the strategy that the situation required. To these can be added twelve other instances in which the initiative for taking an important military measure came, as far as one can see, from him.[7]

Mr. Roosevelt Takes the Reins and Drives: 1939–1941

As early as July, 1939, Mr. Roosevelt issued a Military Order that moved the Joint Board of the Army and Navy, the body co-ordinating their strategic plans; the Army-Navy Munitions Board, the agency controlling their procurement programs; and the civilian office then in charge of military production, into the Executive Office of the President, an institution then newly formed and now so conspicuous a feature of the Government.[8] This order made the Chiefs of Staff, as members of the Joint Board, directly responsible to him. Nothing could signify more clearly that Mr. Roosevelt intended to wield the military power of the United States with his own hands, and not through the Secretaries of War and Navy. Mr. Stimson had very little to do with strategy during the war, except in the role of vigorous counselor and respected elder statesman, as he himself has told us;[9] and Secretary Knox had even less. From the date of the Military Order of 1939 until Pearl Harbor, F.D.R. made all of his important decisions regarding the use of American military power either independently of his military chiefs, or against their advice and over their protests; and this was the period in which the kind of war the United States was going to fight, as well as the weapons with which we were to fight it, was determined.

It is enough to list some of these decisions to feel their weight:

1. His order, in November, 1938, for the creation of plant capacity to produce 10,000 combat airplanes a year, which in May, 1940, during the German *blitz* in France, he stepped up to 50,000 a year. He did this over the protests of the Army and Navy chiefs that these orders would hopelessly unbalance the re-armament of their services.[10]

2. His order, in June, 1940, to give all-out military assistance to Britain. The Army and Navy, believing then that Britain was doomed, protested that this policy would leave the United States stripped of the arms it would need if forced to fight alone. They urged instead: no more war materials for the Allies; a defensive policy in the Pacific; and mobilization for hemisphere defense.[11] Mr. Roosevelt overrode their protests, as he did their similar protests against lend-lease to the Soviet Union and China in 1941.[12]

3. His decision in July, 1941, against the advice of General George C. Marshall, War Department Chief of Staff, and Admiral Harold R. Stark, then Chief of Naval Operations, to clamp an oil embargo on Japan, and to defend and reinforce the Philippines, though all War Department plans had assumed that the Philippines were indefensible.[13]

4. In this same spring and summer his decision, against the advice of General Marshall and Lt. Gen. Stanley D. Embick, his senior military adviser, to establish garrisons and convoys in the western Atlantic.[14]

These decisions were a legitimate performance of the President's constitutional duty. It was a reasonable one if we assume, as I think one must, that during this period the policy of the President was to find an alternative to war rather than to prepare the nation to fight a war. This was his declared purpose in giving all-out aid short of war to Britain, China, and the U.S.S.R., at the expense of our own military preparations. What he wanted, and quickly, was not primarily rearmament, but a demonstration of his determination to mobilize and use America's enormous war potential, in the hope that this might save Great Britain, deter Japan, and make war unnecessary.[15] On the other hand, although he overrode the judgment of the War and Navy Departments regarding rearmament and regarding the immediate application of their meager forces, he directed them to develop, in secret conversations with the British, plans for the war they would have to fight if the deterrent failed.[16] He studied these strategic plans and laid them aside, without approval or disapproval, though he later made their basic principles his own.[17] His policy of deterrence by a display of power was a costly gamble that failed, and on December 7, 1941, we found ourselves in the two-front war which the military experts had warned Mr. Roosevelt we would be unprepared to fight. But largely thanks to Mr. Roosevelt we had never before in our history entered a war with such a well-concerted program of strategy. And thanks again to his initiative the Army and Navy had produced in the fall of 1941, programs of war production, the so-called "Victory Program," designed to enable the United States and Great Britain to crush the Axis and Japan into surrender even if Soviet Russia was knocked out of the war.[18] "Rainbow 5"—the Army-Navy strategic plan that went into effect on 7 December 1941—outlined with remarkable prescience the program of strategy by which the Allies brought the war to a victorious conclusion. And the Victory Program took the measure of the immense effort of production which American industry would have to gird itself to support.

The Period of Hostilities

It can be argued that those students of Mr. Roosevelt who have emphasized his unwillingness to interfere with his military chiefs were not referring to the prewar period, but to the period of declared hostilities, the three and a half years after Pearl Harbor. At first glance it would seem that in this period Mr. Roosevelt, with only one or two notable exceptions, kept his hand off of the military machine, and certainly that he exercised much less influence in shaping American strategy than Mr. Churchill exercised in shaping British, and for that matter Allied strategy.

In striking contrast with Mr. Churchill, Mr. Roosevelt seemed to be content, once the United States had entered the war, to leave his military chiefs free to work out their own strategic ideas, subject to his general direction and approval; and to intervene only very rarely and then as a mediator between conflicting views. Mr. Churchill, on the other hand, was notoriously articulate and active in arguing for his concepts not only of strategy, but of tactics, weapons, equipment, and every other aspect of the British military effort by land, by sea, and in the air; and pressing these on his associates in the Government and on commanders in the field, at all hours of the day and night.[19]

Mr. Roosevelt's Decisive Interventions

It is easy to overdo this contrast, which cannot be reconciled with facts that are of record. Of the cases noted in which F.D.R. overruled his military chiefs, more than half of the twenty-odd (instead of Sherwood's two) can be cited as having occurred in 1942, 1943, and 1944. And this reckoning does not include the cases in which the Joint Chiefs of Staff probably refrained from proposing a plan which represented their best military judgment, because they knew that they could not get Mr. Roosevelt to support it.[20]

But if Mr. Roosevelt exercised a more positive control over the military conduct of the war than is immediately apparent, it was mainly in 1942 and 1943 that this was true. In 1944–45, with one important exception—the relief of General Stilwell in October, 1944—he backed his Joint Chiefs one hundred percent.[21] Regarding 1944–45, but only regarding this period, one can agree with Professor Ehrman that "American strategy emerged from the White House much as it had emerged from the Pentagon." [22]

Four major decisions in the 1942–43 period in which Mr. Roosevelt reversed the judgment of the Joint Chiefs of Staff were:

(1) the decision for TORCH in July, 1942;

(2) Mr. Roosevelt's decision in March, 1943, to allot

American ships to Britain to sustain its non-military imports from overseas at the rate of 27 million tons a year;

(3) his intervention at the TRIDENT Conference in May, 1943, to reduce the scale of the cross-Channel attack;

(4) his decision at Cairo in November, 1943, to cancel BUCCANEER, an amphibious assault in the Bay of Bengal, in support of the 1944 campaign in Burma.

Mr. Roosevelt's decision for TORCH in July, 1942, diverted to an invasion of North Africa all the American forces then available, including those that the War Department had since April been shipping to England for an invasion of the continent in 1943.[23] This decision changed the course that American military policy had taken, and it fixed the frame within which American strategy during 1943 had to be worked out.

In March, 1942, the Joint Chiefs had come forward with their plan for the concentration of Allied forces in England for a massive cross-Channel blow in the spring of 1943, to knock Germany out of the war. Mr. Roosevelt adopted it. In April the British accepted it, and preparations began. But the plan included a rider, SLEDGEHAMMER, about which the British at once began to express doubt and anxiety. SLEDGEHAMMER was a raid in force that the Allies were to launch in September, 1942, under one of two critical conditions: (1) if the Russians were about to cave in; or (2) in the unlikely event that the Germans showed signs of cracking up. The British concluded that SLEDGEHAMMER would be a risk that the Allies could not afford to take, and withdrew their support from this feature of the plan. The Joint Chiefs were in a weak position on this issue since the British would have to provide most of the force to be risked. But they insisted, and the result was a deadlock. In July Mr. Roosevelt broke it. He sent General Marshall, Admiral King and Harry Hopkins to London with instructions to get an agreement with the British either on SLEDGEHAMMER, or on some other plan that would commit large American ground forces to action in Europe before the end of 1942. He signed these instructions: "Franklin Delano Roosevelt, Commander-in-Chief." [24]

SLEDGEHAMMER, the rock on which the Anglo-American agreement on strategy foundered, was a subordinate feature of the American plan. What the American military chiefs wanted above all was commitment to a full-bodied cross-Channel blow at Germany in the spring of 1943. This the British had given without reservations. Why then did the Americans insist on SLEDGEHAMMER as essential? It would seem clearly to have been because Mr. Roosevelt had signified as early as December, 1941, and repeatedly thereafter, that he wanted American ground forces committed to action in Europe before the end of 1942, and the Joint Chiefs could present no acceptable alternative to SLEDGEHAMMER to meet Mr. Roosevelt's demand.[25] TORCH was an alternative acceptable to the British, but not to the American strategists. Mr. Roosevelt ordered its adoption. He had, as was soon realized, cut the ground out from under ROUNDUP in 1943, as well as SLEDGEHAMMER.

Did this mean that the President had been half-hearted, if not disingenuous, in his support of the American plan and from the first preferred Mr. Churchill's Mediterranean strategy to concentration for a blow from England in 1943? Mr. Stimson thought so. This, he wrote, was the President's "great secret baby," and his intimation was that it had been placed on Mr. Roosevelt's doorstep by Mr. Churchill.[26] But in the lack of more convincing testimony on this than Mr. Stimson's there is no reason to believe that Mr. Roosevelt had committed himself to ROUNDUP with his fingers crossed. He had sent General Marshall and Harry Hopkins to England in April to urge it on Churchill and he used freely his authority at home to give priority to the build-up in England.

Mr. Roosevelt's openly declared position was that offensive action in Europe by major American ground forces in 1942 should take precedence over concentration for an offensive in 1943, if the two objectives were found to be inconsistent. It must be borne in mind that, in the circumstances of 1942, his insistence on this had a bearing on one of the cardinal principles of joint strategy to which the Americans had pledged their loyalty, namely, that Germany was the Number One enemy. That, Mr. Roosevelt was too astute a politician not to see. In 1942, the war against Japan was the war to which the emotions of the American public were committed. Strong popular support of the war against the Axis could be counted on only when American troops came to grips with the enemy on the battlefields of Europe.

The idea that Mr. Roosevelt had substituted an English for an American concept of strategy took root in the Pentagon. It developed into the notion that he had accepted a strategy of indecisive encirclement and had repudiated the strategy of a body-blow at the Germans from England. At the TRIDENT Conference in May, 1943, and even later, the American Chiefs felt that they must win the President back to this strategy and then make sure that he remained firm in his support of it.[27] But their anxiety is the only evidence that he had ever deserted it. In 1943, as the conditions for its success ripened, he used his influence in favor of its execution in the spring of 1944. In time his military advisers came to realize the merits of the postponement. A massive attack from England in the spring of 1943 would have staked everything on one shot. And postponement permitted the development of an American strategy more appropriate to a global two-front war, one that brought almost simultaneous victory over both Japan and Germany.

Mr. Roosevelt's substitution of his own strategy for that of his military chiefs in the case of TORCH is well known. His rejection of their judgment on meeting the British import crisis has only recently been brought into full view.[28]

As everyone knows, the British economy in war and peace depends for its very existence on an uninterrupted flow of imports. By 1942, the U-boat had cut this vital input from a prewar annual average of 50 million tons to 23 million tons. The British saw themselves approaching the brink of disaster, notwithstanding the drastic curtailment they had imposed on domestic consumption and services, and in November, 1942, they asked the American Government, in the interest of the common war effort, for the loan of enough ships to bring imports in 1943 up to the minimum needed for their survival at fighting strength. This they estimated as 27 million tons. The President promptly promised to meet their requirement with American shipping, and directed Admiral Land, Chairman of the Maritime Commission, to provide it. On November 30, he assured Mr.

Churchill that United States shipping would not be diverted from the import program "without his personal approval."

By the end of 1942, the situation had grown even worse than the British had anticipated in November. Support of the North African campaign had required more cargo ships, and more of these had been sunk by submarines, than had been expected. In the last quarter of 1942, imports were coming into Britain at an annual rate of only 20 million instead of 23 million tons.

The Joint Chiefs were not informed of the President's promise to Mr. Churchill until late in December, and then only "very unofficially and confidentially" by the British staff mission in Washington. They seem not to have taken it seriously enough. A month later, at the Allied conference at Casablanca, they agreed with the British chiefs on operations in 1943 that would require 6 million more tons of cargo shipping than could be obtained except at the expense of the British import program. But the British went home from Casablanca assuming that the President's promise would nevertheless be kept.

Not until nearly seven weeks later, in March, did the fog of misunderstanding lift enough for the parties concerned to see that they were on a collision course, and by this time the shipping crisis had mounted to a point that portended calamity. In February, Rommel had broken through the American defenses in Tunisia, and in March the sinking of ships in the Atlantic was mounting toward a new and portentous high. The Joint Chiefs then decided to confront the President with the choice between seeing all the military operations to which the Allies had committed themselves for 1943, with his approval, grind to a halt, or cutting into British imports. On April 10, they officially confronted him with their view.

They were two weeks too late. In mid-March, Mr. Churchill had sent his Foreign Secretary, Sir Anthony Eden, to Washington to get an understanding and action. The President, without consulting the military, directed Harry Hopkins, and Lewis Douglas, chief of the War Shipping Administration, to find enough shipping to carry out his pledge. Douglas, convinced that the military services were wasting the shipping space under their control (and sharing Hopkins' concern over their anti-British attitude), advised Mr. Roosevelt that his order could be carried out without crippling their strategic program. It was. The outcome was, in part a vindication of Mr. Roosevelt's jaunty conviction that people can do more than they think possible if they have to; in part it was due to the sudden triumph, in April, of the Allied war on the submarine, in time to justify Mr. Roosevelt's optimistic gamble. After March, ship losses fell off rapidly, and new construction began to exceed expectations. When the Allies met at Quebec in August, shipping deficits were a thing of the past. Meanwhile, in May, Mr. Roosevelt had topped off handsomely his pledge to Churchill by directing the transfer to the British of fifteen to twenty ships a month for the next ten months.[29]

The incident illustrates the loose co-ordination of the American war effort that characterized Mr. Roosevelt as an administrator. But his pledge meant that he was making his own decisions regarding the use of American military resources; and his execution of it, against the protest of his military advisers, signified his determination to keep American military efforts loyally aligned with our strategic commitments to the British.

In handling the TORCH decision Mr. Roosevelt's method had been to confront his military chiefs, step by step, with the facts that made his decision the only practicable alternative. His intervention at the Allied conference in May, 1943 (TRIDENT), shows him using a different method of imposing his strategic views.

The Joint Chiefs having, as they felt, "lost their shirts" to the British at Casablanca, in January, went to the TRIDENT Conference, in May, elaborately prepared to pin the British down to a cross-Channel attack in the spring of 1944.[30] We know that they briefed Mr. Roosevelt before the conference, and they must have informed him that they were going to insist on a powerful assault of ROUNDUP proportions.[31] Whether he argued with them about this we do not know. We only know that he could not have supported them without risking a breach with the British, which he would be sure not to tolerate, or else by ordering the Navy, against its will, to produce for Europe tank-landing ships (LST's) which Admiral King would need in 1944 to launch his offensive through the Central Pacific and bring the Air Forces within bombing distance of Japan. That, Mr. Roosevelt chose not to do. He may have given more weight than his military chiefs to the limitations on war production which the outcome of the "feasibility" dispute with the War Production Board had recently revealed.[32] In any case, what he did, in his opening remarks at the TRIDENT Conference, was to declare his opinion that the Allies might have to settle for a cross-Channel attack in the spring of 1944, on the scale of SLEDGEHAMMER rather than ROUNDUP.

He had made a more realistic guess than his military experts as to what would be practicable. A study by the Americans of the figures submitted by the British (who had brought with them a plan for an even heavier assault than the Americans proposed) left no doubt that only a modest assault force could be launched in the following spring unless a much larger assault lift could be provided. The American Chiefs were in an awkward position, since only they could provide the types of assault craft (in particular, LST's) needed for the more massive assault to which they wished to commit the British; and these they were not willing to promise. The President had let them go out on a limb that did not support their weight. Adjusting themselves to the facts, they accepted as the only reasonable step under the circumstances, a decision of the Combined Chiefs to begin planning for an assault on a more modest scale, and with built-in conditions (ROUNDHAMMER), which General Marshall described as "something more than SLEDGEHAMMER and less than ROUNDUP"—this plus a promise from the British to permit the transfer of seven divisions from the Mediterranean to England in November, 1943.[33]

Finally, let us take a look at the decision to cancel BUCCANEER.[34] Mr. Roosevelt made it at Cairo on 5 December 1943, after the British and American chiefs had come back from their meeting with Stalin at Tehran. The operation was part of a painfully concocted scheme to bring Chiang Kai-shek's ground forces into action in Burma and reopen the Burma Road. The American Chiefs had worked it out in the desperate hope of salvaging the Allies' military policy in China, which Mr. Roosevelt had repeatedly taken into his own hands against the firm and outspoken advice of

General Marshall and Secretary Stimson. The British did not like the plan for Burma, but the Joint Chiefs had induced them to accept it. At Cairo, Chiang Kai-shek, on the use of whose forces in Burma the success of the plan depended, agreed to co-operate, but only on condition that the Allies would launch an amphibious attack on the Andaman Islands simultaneously with the invasion of Burma. This was BUCCANEER. In an expansive moment during a conversation with Chiang at Cairo, before he and Mr. Churchill went to Tehran to discuss strategy with Stalin, Mr. Roosevelt promised Chiang BUCCANEER.

Nothing the President did during the war was more embarrassing to his military chieftains. The Joint Chiefs were not consulted about his pledge to Chiang; they were not even directly informed of it but learned of it through "the grapevine." BUCCANEER could be undertaken only with fifteen of the few and precious LST's on which the execution of a spring OVERLORD depended. A week later, at Tehran, Mr. Roosevelt committed himself also to a May OVERLORD which was the dearest object of their strategy. This put the American Chiefs in the impossible position vis-à-vis the British of having, in dutiful support of their Commander-in-Chief, to insist firmly on BUCCANEER even though they —and the British—knew that this would make a spring OVERLORD impracticable, and probably rule it out as an operation at any time in 1944. At the last minute Mr. Roosevelt reluctantly gave in and asked Chiang to release him from his promise, as the Joint Chiefs, with the exception of Admiral King wished.[35]

But in his handling of BUCCANEER he parted company with them for all but the last time. From January, 1944, until his death—with the one exception previously mentioned, the recall of Stilwell—he not only let them run the war, but backed them with the full weight of his authority even against the British.

The decision for TORCH, which the Joint Chiefs had accepted with dismay and unconcealed dissatisfaction, set the stage on which the drama of American strategy in Europe, and in the Pacific as well, was to be played out. No one can question the fact that Mr. Roosevelt set the stage. But it is generally believed that having done so he left the American Chiefs free to get their way with the British, and that, beginning with TRIDENT, he firmly supported them, except in the case of BUCCANEER. His action at TRIDENT mentioned above is a challenge to this view. There is, indeed, considerable evidence to support the thesis that the realistic form that American strategy took during 1943, as contrasted with the strategy which the American Chiefs insistently contended for with the British, was shaped throughout by Mr. Roosevelt's hand.

What was this actual American strategy?

American Strategy and its Determinants

The situation in January, 1943, imposed on both Allies two tasks to which without hesitation they gave first claim on their combined resources. One was their campaign to quell the U-boat menace and regain control of their communications with each other and with Russia. The other was unstinting aid to the Russians to keep them killing Germans. Also the Americans willingly—the U.S. Air Forces eagerly—sent their heavy bombers to England to join the

Royal Air Force in blasting and burning the vitals of the Axis war economy and striking at their enemies' will to fight. The Combined Bomber Offensive was given until April, 1944, to achieve air supremacy over Europe as a condition preliminary to a cross-Channel attack on 1 May 1944, on which the Allies agreed, though as yet only in principle.

As for the Mediterranean, the Allies, in January, 1943, were on the defensive in Tunisia, and the Americans were committed to their share of the task of driving the Germans and Italians from the north shore of Africa. This the Allies accomplished in May, 1943. The Americans had agreed at Casablanca to join, once that was done, in such further operations as were necessary to clear the Mediterranean as a line of communications with the Middle East, with Russia (via the Persian Gulf), and with the Far East. To this end the Americans had agreed to an invasion of Sicily in July. This shook the Italian government, which began to feel its way toward surrender. To make sure of its surrender, and recognizing the strategic advantages of a swift occupation of Italy to which this might lead, the Americans committed themselves to an invasion of the mainland. When the Nazis unexpectedly decided to hold Italy and committed a force to defend their position there, the American military chiefs were ready to join in a powerful campaign against them, accepting the argument that this would pin down and bleed the Germans in Italy while the Allies were building enough strength in England for a power-drive across the Channel in the spring of 1944. But they exercised a steadily increasing pressure on the British to limit this, and other operations in the Mediterranean, in favor of that build-up.

In these decisions to go along with the British the Americans were returning to the original agreement of the Allies that their initial strategy should be to close a ring around Nazi-occupied Europe and tighten it until they were ready to knock Germany out by a blow to the solar plexus. The area in which American strategy departed sharply from that on which the Allies had originally decided was in the Pacific. In their original program of strategy they had agreed merely to contain the Japanese until the Allies had defeated the Axis. But in 1943, the Americans, seeing no prospect of a body-blow at Germany before 1944, and even that a questionable possibility, went over to the offensive in the Pacific, merely notifying the British that they found it necessary to do so. After Guadalcanal they struck for the great naval and air bastion that the Japanese had built up at Rabaul, and before the end of the year Admiral King and Admiral Nimitz were readying forces for a power-drive through the Central Pacific. And the Joint Chiefs persistently, though vainly, tried to get a land campaign launched in Burma to reopen the Burma Road into China.

Such, very briefly, was American strategy in the critical year 1943. Except for the first three items mentioned—the anti-U-boat campaign, aid to Russia, and the bomber offensive—it was not the strategy the the American Joint Chiefs (except Admiral King) wanted. What the Army planners, responsible for European strategy tried to get was an overriding commitment to a cross-Channel attack in the spring of 1944. Once the Mediterranean had been cleared as a line of communication, they would, at first, have liked to put the Mediterranean theater on a caretaker status and transfer the bulk of its forces to England. They adjusted, though on conditions, to maintaining the Mediterranean as a scene of major activity when they saw that this might be turned to account in support of OVERLORD.

But, with the same three exceptions, neither was the strategy followed what Mr. Churchill and the British Chiefs wanted. They regarded the American offensives in the Pacific with anxiety and suspicion, and they resented and fought the tightening restraints imposed on operations in the Mediterranean in the interest of a cross-Channel power-drive.

The strategy of the Allies, then, in 1943, the year in which it became fixed by the deployment of their military resources, was not what it would have been if the American Joint Chiefs had had their way, or if the British had had their way. It crystallized out of compromises between the American Joint Chiefs and the British, and within the Joint Chiefs of Staff between the Army, the Air Forces, and the Navy, in a sequence of realistic adjustments to changing conditions. But the timing and balance of the compromises was determined by Mr. Roosevelt.

Let me illustrate.

When the Allies met at Casablanca in January, 1943, to decide on their tasks for the year, the American Chiefs had not got over the disappointment and disarray into which TORCH had thrown their hopes and plans, and they went to the conference without agreement, among themselves, on a new program.[36] Mr. Roosevelt therefore called the tunes. To them he appeared to be all too ready to do whatever Mr. Churchill and the British Chiefs wanted done. But let the fact not be overlooked that as early as November, 1942, as soon as the Allies had gone ashore in Africa, it was Mr. Roosevelt who took the initiative in encouraging Mr.

Churchill's brightest hopes for concentration in the Mediterranean, proposing that he have the Combined Chiefs explore the possibilities of "forward movement directed against Sardinia, Sicily, Italy, Greece and other Balkan [please note, "Balkan"] areas, and including the possibility of obtaining Turkish support for an attack through the Black Sea against Germany's flank." [37] But at the Casablanca Conference the American Joint Chiefs put a damper on ambitious plans for "forward" movement in the Mediterranean by serving notice on the British that the United States must exert increasing pressure on the Japanese. This was a deviation from the agreed strategy of containment in the Pacific until Germany was defeated. The British were alarmed and protested, but they acquiesced.[38] They would hardly have done so had they not known that Mr. Roosevelt was in favor of the deviation.

Mr. Roosevelt's intervention at the next Allied Conference—TRIDENT, in May, 1943—cutting his military chiefs' pattern for ROUNDUP down to manageable size, has already been described.

Three months later, about to meet the British again at Quebec, the American Army Chiefs prepared more grimly than ever to get from them an unequivocal commitment to "overriding priority" for a cross-Channel attack on May 1, 1944. But perhaps remembering TRIDENT, General Marshall took the precaution of having his chief planner, General Handy, fly to Washington from Quebec to see Mr. Roosevelt before the conference opened. When the President arrived at Quebec the next day "it was already clear," to quote the official historian, "that a compromise was in the making and that the U.S. staff would have to accept something less than 'overriding priority'." [39] What the

Combined Chiefs decided, with Mr. Roosevelt's—and Mr. Churchill's—approval was to pass from planning to definite preparations for OVERLORD based on the plan submitted by COSSAC, but without removing the conditions built into that plan, or authorizing a stronger assault, though Mr. Churchill now wished to increase its strength by twenty-five percent.

Even at Cairo-Tehran in December, the showdown conferences for 1944, when Mr. Roosevelt evidently believed that OVERLORD could and should be executed in the spring, and the American chiefs were on tenterhooks about the willingness of the British to see it through, Mr. Roosevelt retained a wait-and-see attitude until Stalin had spoken, and throughout the conversations with Stalin and the British he remained much more open-minded and flexible than his military chiefs regarding the exact timing of the invasion, and even regarding the possibility of further operations in the Mediterranean.[40]

The Pacific, the Cross-Channel Invasion, and Mr. Roosevelt

The strategic issue that Mr. Roosevelt handled with the closest attention to timing and balance in 1942–43 was the competing claims of the Mediterranean and the Pacific. In the summer of 1942, when the British withdrew their support from SLEDGEHAMMER, Admiral King became convinced that they would never support a strong cross-Channel attack, and he and General Marshall had gone to F.D.R. with the proposal that the United States go all out in the Pacific. Mr. Roosevelt came down hard on them with a flat "no." [41] They must stick to the principle that Germany was the Number One enemy; and no good reason has been presented for doubting that there and thereafter, Mr. Roosevelt was as convinced as they were that a direct and massive invasion would be necessary to defeat Germany. But at Casablanca he let Admiral King serve notice that the United States must go over to the offensive against Japan, and as American resources became more abundant, Mr. Roosevelt let more and more of these go to the Pacific.

Mr. Roosevelt adhered to this policy in spite of the strain it put on our relations with the British, and the anxiety it gave to the War Department. He omitted landing craft from his famous list of "must" goals for war production in 1943 —an omission at the moment gratifying to Admiral King, who did not wish his shipyards to be diverted from the construction of a new fleet with which to overpower the Japanese in the western Pacific.[42] In March, 1943, when the British pressed the Joint Chiefs to order the construction of LST's, without which a 1944 ROUNDUP would be impossible, their plea was met with suspicion and Admiral King was allowed to block it.[43] At TRIDENT Mr. Roosevelt let Admiral King and the Joint Chiefs get the policy of Pacific offensives written into the books of the Combined Chiefs. Even at QUADRANT, when the availability of LST's for OVERLORD had become a burning issue, Mr. Roosevelt, though he came out strongly for a cross-Channel attack in the spring of 1944, made no visible move to have the production of LST's increased or, later, to change the allocation that gave Admiral King first call on the LST's that the Navy's shipyards began to launch in October.

But all this does not mean that he had abandoned the

strategy of defeating Germany first, or ceased to believe that a cross-Channel body-blow would be necessary. He let Admiral King and General MacArthur have the means to step up their offensives against Japan, but he kept his hand on the brake. When Admiral King had followed up the TORCH decision in July, 1942, by pressing at once for reinforcement of the Pacific, Mr. Roosevelt supported the War Department in resisting—at least until it was certain that TORCH would make ROUNDUP in 1943 impossible.[44] On October 24, 1942, he ordered the Joint Chiefs to hold Guadalcanal at all costs, even if this meant delay in fulfilling other commitments, including those made to the British. This decision alarmed General Arnold, then in the midst of his struggle with the Navy to prevent the transfer of his heavy bombers from England to the Pacific. It could, he has observed, have "changed completely our planning for strategic operations against Germany." [45] But Mr. Roosevelt at the same time directed that the top priorities assigned to production for the war in Europe remain in effect.[46] Historians of the war have said of Mr. Roosevelt that he was "tardily converted to BOLERO" (i.e. to a cross-Channel invasion).[47] But I have seen no convincing evidence that he needed conversion or ever abandoned the stand that he took on July 13, 1942, in his instructions to Harry Hopkins when he was about to send him to England to get a decision for action in 1942 in Europe: "Under any circumstances I wish BOLERO and ROUNDUP to remain an essential objective, even though it must be interrupted." [48]

What alarmed General Marshall and his planners more and more, as time passed without a definitive commitment to a firmly dated assault in force, was their conviction that

OVERLORD required a scheduled production of munitions and equipment reaching back through the whole intricate complex of war industry and, in the case of specialized items, involving a time-lag of up to eighteen months.[49] Mr. Roosevelt was certainly aware of this. Yet he calmly pursued his policy and took the risk. What his motives were one can only conjecture. Noting that he began more clearly to favor a 1944 OVERLORD only at Quebec in August, 1943, it is to be observed that by that date two conditions had been met: (1) the U-boats had been driven from the Atlantic sea-lanes; and (2) the American war economy, now fully mobilized, was pouring out materiel of all kinds in an abundance that exceeded the most sanguine expectations.[50] If the American military chiefs had had their way and had got a cross-Channel attack delivered in 1943, Allied strategy would have staked everything on a very dangerous gamble. By the summer of 1943 the Allies were entering a period of plenty and they could play for high stakes with far more assurance of the outcome.

Mr. Roosevelt liked to play by ear. But it is permissible to argue that the concept underlying his guidance of American strategy was that the role of America was from first to last to serve as "the arsenal of Democracy," and that its proper contribution to victory was to confront its enemies with a rapidly growing weight of material power that they could not hope to match; then use it to crush them with a minimum expenditure of American lives. This conjecture is confirmed by the timing of his gradual alteration of course to firmer support for the execution of OVERLORD, for which his military advisers consistently contended.

As early as January, 1941, when his military staff were about to enter into the secret "ABC" conversations with the British, he laid down two principles for their guidance: (1) ". . . our military course must be very conservative until our strength [has] developed"; and (2) ". . . we must be ready to act with what is available." [51] Only when a preponderance of military power had been established could strategy safely be allowed to crystallize. It was not until the end of 1943, that "war production in many categories had caught up with the demand." [52] But by the summer of 1943, abundance was readily foreseeable. While it was being achieved it had been prudent to tailor strategic programs to the availability of finished munitions and equipment. But now, with war production in high gear, we had enough power in munitions and shipping to use decisively on more than one major front. The problem of firm advance planning of the necessary types of arms and equipment still worried the American military chiefs and continued to give the British a bad opinion of them as being "rigid" planners. But it had ceased to be critical. Mr. Roosevelt did not finally authorize his chiefs to concentrate this potential against Germany until after the conference with Stalin at Tehran in November, 1943. But I find it reasonable to believe that his increasingly outspoken support of a full-out cross-Channel assault in the spring and summer of 1943 was governed by his knowledge that he was acquiring the power to make it decisive without scanting other important objectives. If he was jaunty about the one item that was still in critically short supply, namely, assault landing craft for OVERLORD, this was in accord with his conviction, repeatedly expressed, that if the military really needed something that they wanted, they could find it; and the event proved that he was right.[53]

Indirectness and Consistency

We are left to conjecture about this, as about so many other of Mr. Roosevelt's moves and motives, because of his characteristic preference for getting things done by indirection. He seldom declared his motives, and unlike Mr. Churchill, he did not thresh things out with his advisers. He disliked and avoided argument with them and preferred to work in ways that were highly irregular and personal. Marshall and King had direct access to him, and he called them to the White House (sometimes when he was in bed), whenever he felt a need for their counsel.[54] But he listened to advice only when he chose, and he sought it only on occasion.[55] General Marshall came to seem to him indispensable as an adviser. In January, 1944, he said to him, to explain his decision to make Eisenhower the Supreme Commander of the Allied Expeditionary Force; "I feel I could not sleep at night with you out of the country." [56] But at one time, in the thick of the war, General Marshall told Alan Brooke that he had not seen the President for two weeks. The one measure that Mr. Roosevelt took to establish regular liaison with the Joint Chiefs of Staff was to appoint Admiral Leahy as Chief of Staff to the President, and also Chairman of the Joint Chiefs. This supplied a reliable and serviceable but imperfect link.[57] Much more effectual was the influence of the President's alter ego, Harry Hopkins, who became an invisible member of the Joint Chiefs, indeed of the Combined Chiefs of Staff.[58] But it is evident that to the end of the period 1942–43, during which Mr. Roosevelt was exercising a decisive control over American strategy, his military chiefs did not anticipate some of his most important decisions. Some of these were purely negative, for, as Professor Emerson has pointed out, he had learned from a long career in politics that one way to decide is to do nothing.[59] In general, Mr. Roosevelt showed more confidence in the logic of events than in close planning in advance. He was disposed to let things happen instead of giving orders, when he saw that they were likely to happen as he wished. And as often as not, when the experts confronted him with a conflict between a military end and a declared insufficiency of means, he breezily ordered both his military chiefs and his production chiefs to do what was necessary, always confident that they could do more than they declared to be possible.[60] Until he had made up his mind he played his cards close to his chest. But when he made up his mind he made it up hard. Admiral Leahy has told us how Mr. Roosevelt would say to him after he had presented views of the Joint Chiefs with which F.D.R.'s were not in agreement: "I am a pig-headed Dutchman, Bill, and I have made up my mind about this. We are going ahead with this and you can't change my mind." [61]

Given Mr. Roosevelt's ways of getting things done, and with no such memoirs as Mr. Churchill's to assist them, historians have had almost as much difficulty in tracing the course of Mr. Roosevelt's influence on the military direction of America's war effort as the Joint Chiefs had in anticipating his decisions. But one certainly cannot say, given the record, that he had any compunctions about overriding —or ignoring—the counsels of his military experts, or agree with Mr. Churchill that he was "oppressed by the prejudices of his military advisers."

The principles that guided him as war leader of the American nation, and his determination to follow them, he made clear at an early date, and if the military chiefs had difficulties in foreseeing what practical application he would give them, they could have no doubt that he would overrule any proposal or measure of theirs that in his judgment conflicted with these principles. They can be summarized as follows:

1. The solidarity of the Anglo-American coalition must be maintained for military reasons, and also because the interest of the United States required the survival of Great Britain and its postwar freedom of action as a great power.

2. Nazi Germany is the Number One enemy and must be defeated and crushed at the earliest possible date.

3. Soviet Russia must be given unstinted aid and kept fighting to the end.[62]

4. Germany and Japan must be forced to unconditional surrender.

5. China must be kept in the war, with the object of having it enter the postwar world as a great power.

6. The interest of the United States in the postwar world requires an international organization of "United Nations," and this, to establish itself, must at first be directed by a

firm union of the victorious allies: the United States, Great
Britain and its Commonwealth, the U.S.S.R., and China.

These were political as well as military objectives. What
is important in a study of Mr. Roosevelt as Commander-in-
Chief is that the decisions he made to achieve these objectives—with the glaring exception of China—made military
sense.

In the case of China Mr. Roosevelt consistently substituted his judgment for that of both his military chiefs and
the British. The military policies that he dictated for that
theater of war ended in dismal failure.

On the credit side is the shape that he gave to American
and Allied strategy for the defeat of the Axis in Europe,
and Japan in the Pacific. The Americans agreed from the
start that the main effort of the United States must first be
thrown into the defeat of Germany, and that this must be
complete. But how? No evidence has been adduced for the
suspicion that, in the spring of 1942, when the War Department came up with its BOLERO-ROUNDUP plan, Mr. Roosevelt backed it half-heartedly, or that after TORCH he had to
be won over to the view that a body-blow at Germany delivered from England by a force of combined arms would
be necessary. The practically important question was the
timing of the blow, and making maximum and aggressive
use of what we had until we had accumulated enough power
to deliver a knock-out punch. Mr. Roosevelt saw that this
was the issue sooner and more clearly than his military advisers. In the course of 1943, when that power seemed at
last to be in hand, Mr. Roosevelt showed himself more and
more clearly to be in favor of delivering the punch in the

spring of 1944. His use of the delay had kept us with the British, had cleared the Mediterranean, had brought about the overthrow of Mussolini and the surrender of Italy, had thrown the Germans on the defensive, had begun the crippling of their air force and their war industries, and had given us seasoned troops and commanders. It had meanwhile permitted Mr. Roosevelt to let the Navy and General MacArthur get well along with the business of defeating the Japanese, while the Allies were bringing to a head the strength to give OVERLORD a reasonable chance of success. In short, thanks largely to Mr. Roosevelt's exercise of his military authority, the United States had developed a strategy appropriate to a two-front war on a global scale, which brought Japan to terms within a few months after the unconditional surrender of Germany, and without the redeployment of our forces.

Appendix
to
Chapter III

FRANKLIN D. ROOSEVELT: COMMANDER-IN-CHIEF

A. Decisions of F.D.R. against the advice, or over the protests, of his military advisers:

1938–1941

NOVEMBER, 1938—Ordered production of 10,000 airplanes within two years, and creation of plant capacity to produce 10,000 a year, a figure raised to 50,000 a year. (Watson, *Chief of Staff*, pp. 136–43, 175; AAF History, I, pp. 104, 107: VI, pp. 172, 264.)

JUNE, 1940—Ordered aid to Britain short of war, with munitions, equipment, and supplies regarded by the Army and Navy as necessary to re-arm the United States. (Matloff and Snell, *Strategic Planning, 1941–1942*, pp. 16–21, 29; Emerson, *"F.D.R.,"* p. 144.)

JUNE, 1940—Ordered transfer of B-17's to Britain. (Watson, *Chief of Staff*, p. 306.)

JUNE, 1940—Ordered that the fleet be kept at Pearl Harbor to deter the Japanese. (Matloff and Snell, *Strategic Planning, 1941–1942*, pp. 15–16, 20; Emerson, *"F.D.R.,"* p. 145; S. E. Morison, *The Rising Sun in the Pacific* [Boston: Little Brown and Co., 1948], pp. 46–47.)

MAY, 1941—Ordered lend-lease aid to China. (Matloff and Snell, *Strategic Planning, 1941–1942*, pp. 63–64.)

MAY–JUNE, 1941—Ordered the stationing of garrisons in the Western Atlantic (Matloff and Snell, *Strategic Planning, 1941–1942*, pp. 50–51, 53.)

JULY, 1941—Ordered embargo on shipment of oil to Japan. (Watson, *Chief of Staff*, p. 495; Matloff and Snell, *Strategic Planning, 1941–1942*, pp. 64–65.)

JULY–AUGUST, 1941—Appointed MacArthur and ordered reinforcement of the Philippines. (Matloff and Snell, *Strategic Planning, 1941–1942*, p. 67.)

NOVEMBER, 1941—Approved Hull's ten-point "ultimatum" to Japan. (Watson, *Chief of Staff*, pp. 506–7; Matloff and Snell, *Strategic Planning, 1941–1942*, p. 75; Emerson, *"F.D.R.,"* pp. 146–47.)

1942

MARCH—Directed that lend-lease commitments to the Soviet Union be executed in full and a second Protocol negotiated. (Matloff and Snell, *Strategic Planning, 1941–1942*, pp. 205–7.)

MAY—(Virtually) promised Molotov a second front in 1942, over General Marshall's protest. (Matloff and Snell, *Strategic Planning, 1941–1942*, p. 232.)

MAY–JUNE—Imposed his own plan for reinforcing the British in the Middle East. (Matloff and Snell, *Strategic Planning, 1941–1942*, pp. 246–47. For the background, *ibid.*, pp. 198–202.)

JUNE—Killed Marshall's and King's proposal to go all out in the Pacific. (Matloff and Snell, *Strategic Planning, 1941–1942*, pp. 270–72.)

JULY—Decided to execute TORCH. (Matloff and Snell, *Strategic Planning, 1941–1942*, pp. 273–84.)

AUGUST—Overruled Marshall and his staff regarding the establishment of an air force in the Caucasus. (Matloff and Snell, *Strategic Planning, 1941–1942*, pp. 330–32.)

1943

JANUARY—Overruled the War Department's proposal to make lend-lease to the Soviet Union conditional. (Matloff, *Strategic Planning, 1943–1944*, pp. 281–82.)

MARCH–APRIL—Overruled the JCS on the British import crisis. (Matloff, *Strategic Planning, 1943–1944*, pp. 45–46; Leighton, *Command Decisions*, pp. 199–223.)

MAY—Overrode JCS proposal at TRIDENT on the scale of ROUNDUP. (Richard M. Leighton, MS, "OVERLORD Revisited." *American Historical Review* [July, 1963], pp. 919–37.

MAY—Decided for Chennault against Stilwell over the War Department's protest, and let ANAKIM die. (Matloff, *Strategic Planning, 1943–1944*, pp. 84–88, 124–25.)

AUGUST—Blocked the JCS proposal of a showdown with the British on an overriding priority for OVERLORD. (Matloff, *Strategic Planning, 1943–1944*, pp. 220–23.)

DECEMBER—At the second Cairo Conference reversed himself and overruled the JCS on BUCCANEER. (Matloff, *Strategic Planning, 1943–1944*, pp. 347–53, 369–73.)

1944

OCTOBER—Overrode the judgment of the War Department and Leahy in recalling Stilwell from China. (Matloff, *Strategic Planning, 1943–1944*, p. 477; Charles F. Romanus and Riley Sunderland, *Stilwell's Command Problems* [Washington, 1956, in *U.S. Army in World War II*], pp. 361–471.)

B. Strategic Decisions for which the initiative apparently came from the President:

1941

JANUARY—Issued instructions to the Army and Navy staffs regarding the principles to be observed in the secret (ABC) Anglo-American staff conversations. (Matloff and Snell, *Strategic Planning, 1941–1942*, pp. 28–29.)

JULY—Directed War and Navy Departments to submit production requirements for the defeat of the Axis and Japan. (Watson, *Chief of Staff*, pp. 338–39; Matloff and Snell, *Strategic Planning, 1941–1942*, p. 59.)

1942

JANUARY—Did F.D.R. suggest the [Doolittle] bombing raid on Tokyo, executed in April? (Matloff and Snell, *Strategic Planning, 1941–1942*, p. 139, n. 89; *AAF History*, I, p. 438.)

MARCH—Defined areas of strategic responsibility as between the United States and Great Britain. (Matloff and Snell, *Strategic Planning, 1941–1942*, pp. 166–67.)

APRIL—Ordered the Navy to send *Ranger* to the Indian Ocean

to support Ceylon, and *Washington* and *Wasp* to Scapa
Flow. (Sherwood, *Roosevelt and Hopkins*, p. 534.)

AUGUST—Ordered Army Air Forces to submit estimate of the
number of airplanes necessary to achieve complete air
supremacy over the Axis and Japan. (Arnold, *Global
War*, p. 335.)

NOVEMBER—Promised Churchill American shipping to insure
the British 27,000,000 tons of imports in 1943. (Leighton,
Command Decisions, pp. 199ff.)

NOVEMBER—Suggested to Churchill that the Combined Chiefs
plan for forward movements in the Mediterranean after
victory in Tunisia. (Matloff and Snell, *Strategic Planning, 1941–1942*, p. 363.)

1943

JANUARY—Proposed that he and Churchill seek from Stalin
a definite agreement to join in the war against Japan.
(Matloff, *Strategic Planning, 1943–1944*, p. 32.)

JANUARY—Declared unconditional surrender to be the war aim
of the Allies. (Matloff, *Strategic Planning, 1943–1944*,
p. 37.)

MARCH—Ordered more airplanes for MacArthur to help him
to get to Rabaul. (Matloff, *Strategic Planning, 1943–
1944*, p. 95n [based on Kenney].)

AUGUST—Gave Marshall his plans for further operations in
the Mediterranean, requesting proposals for action rather
than criticisms. (Matloff, *Strategic Planning, 1943–1944*,
pp. 211–12.)

OCTOBER–NOVEMBER—Instructed the War Department, and
asked Churchill, to put punch behind the airlift in Assam,
and (November 10) personally requested Churchill and
Chiang Kai-shek to assist with MATTERHORN (B–29 bombing from bases in China). (Matloff, *Strategic Planning,
1943–1944*, pp. 323, 326.)

IV

AIR POWER
AND STRATEGY

IN THE EVOLUTION OF STRATEGY, as in all the affairs of men, the decisions made and the effect of those decisions are governed largely by feasibility—by conditions determining what, at a given time, it seemed possible to do with the forces in hand; and by the effectiveness of those forces. The strategists of World War II had in hand a new element of force, air power, which in that war rose to a place alongside land and sea power, and transfigured all strategic calculations.

It has been difficult, especially in the United States, to be objective about the role of air power in World War II. Its rapid rise, and the audacious and still untested claims of American air service leaders created sober anxieties as well as an atmosphere of interservice rivalry charged with emotion. Objectivity was difficult for the young and ambitious leaders of the American air forces. It was equally difficult even for historical observers like myself, who were identified during the war with one of the established services. After the war the historians of the air forces achieved it admirably, both in America and in England.[1] They have constructed a basis of fact and judgment for a juster appraisal of air power as an element in the projection and execution of strategy.

A basic fact to be considered in thinking of American

strategy in World War II in terms of the forces created to execute it is the unexpected shape that the combat forces of the United States assumed during the war. The expansion and power of the Navy was no surprise. The relative size of our ground and air forces was. The American combat forces that emerged to fight the decisive battles of 1944–45 had, as previously noted, a compact and powerful but comparatively small ground combat fist. In its Victory Program of September, 1941, the War Department had estimated that the Army would need 215 divisions to defeat the Axis and Japan. But in 1943, General Marshall decided to stop activating divisions when the number reached ninety, and on V-E Day only eighty-nine were in being. And yet the strategy of the Allies, as we have seen, in 1943, finally came to rest on their conclusion that a massive territorial invasion of the continent would be necessary to defeat Germany. After this was launched, in June, 1944, it became their main effort.

This is a consideration of fact. Another consideration basic to seeing the combat effort of the Allies in a just perspective is a consideration of judgment. It cannot reasonably be maintained that air power was the decisive, in the sense of being the major factor, in the defeat of Germany and Japan. But that by its application in a new combination with land and sea power, and in overwhelming force, it became a primary factor in the defeat of both is incontestable. The scrupulously objective experts, who made the United States Strategic Bombing Survey in Europe, were of the opinion that in a matter of months the Allied strategic bombing forces would have produced the surrender of Germany even if the Allies had not crossed the Rhine.[2] The parallel survey of air power in the Pacific reached a similar conclusion regarding the effect of strategic bombing on Japan; but no survey was needed to establish the simple fact that, in combination with naval power, the air forces of the United States forced the Japanese to surrender without an invasion of their homeland by the Army.

How did the American air forces acquire and use the power that enabled them to make these decisive contributions to victory?

The Swift Growth of a Giant

Three months after we got into the war the Army Air Forces, an inexperienced young giant, took its seat beside the Army and Navy at the high table of the American military organization, and in the military councils of the Allies. It had reached this position in swift strides. Three years before it had been only a specialist corps, on a footing with the Signal Corps or the Army Engineers. Three years later it had created the mightiest air force that had ever existed.

This great force originated in the years after World War I, in a branch of the Army's Signal Corps. In 1926 this Air Service had itself become a corps. But until 1938, it remained a stepchild of the War Department. During these years American air power may be said to have existed chiefly as a ferment in the minds of a group of young Army officers who had taken to the air in World War I. This ferment would hardly have captured the attention of the public but for the sensational agitation of General "Billy" Mitchell.

The dream and goal of these young airmen was strategic bombing, and they brought to power with them in 1941–42 a system of doctrine, and a program designed to vindicate their faith in independent air war based on bombing. And by 1936, they had put into production, against the opposition of the Navy, and with the grudging consent of the War Department, a four-engined, long-range bomber, the B–17, the "Flying Fortress," with which they believed that they could make good their claims.[3]

What did they mean by "strategic bombing"?

The term requires definition because it is inexact. It carries a charge of aspiration, if not of boastfulness. It implies that the kind of air offensive to which it refers is the only kind of offensive that is truly strategic. What the term, as used in World War II, actually meant was massive and systematic bombing of the enemy's war economy and of the enemy population's will to resist. Such an offensive would be carried on beyond the reach of ground and sea forces and without their immediate and direct co-operation and support.

The term "strategic" bombing was used to designate this unprecedented kind of warfare because no other acceptable term for it was available.

The event that had broken the shackles of conservative restriction which had bound the Air Corps was one of the prewar initiatives of Mr. Roosevelt, already noted. It was contained in the orders the President issued in November, 1938, and May, 1940, the first directing the Air Corps to produce 10,000 aircraft a year, the second calling for an output of 50,000 a year. "In forty-five minutes," General Arnold, Chief of the War Department's little Air Corps later exclaimed, "I was given $1,500,000,000 and told to get an air force." [4]

After receiving the first of these orders General Arnold had been raised to the position of the Army's Deputy Chief of Staff for Air. Then, in the spring of 1941, Mr. Roosevelt's new Secretary of War, Henry L. Stimson, who, like the President, was convinced that World War II would be "largely an air war," installed in his office an able Assistant Secretary of War for Air, Mr. Robert A. Lovett, to look after his interest in the matter; and on June 21, 1941, the War Department brought into existence "The Army Air Forces," with a general staff of its own, and with Lt. Gen. Henry H. Arnold as its Chief. These adjustments reflected also the views and wishes of General George C. Marshall, who had become the War Department's Chief of Staff, in 1939.

As war came in sight enthusiasts for air-power in the press and Congress, and influential officers of the Air Forces, convinced by their experience with the Army and Navy that they could not achieve their ambition without independence, staged a drive to obtain it. But this was opposed by General Marshall. It was also opposed by General Arnold, provided his staff and forces be given still greater autonomy. The outcome was a truce embodied in a Presidential Order of March 3, 1942, which made the Army Air Forces and the Army Ground Forces the two major combat commands of the Army. During World War II, therefore, the American air force, unlike the British, German, and Italian, was nominally a part of the Army.[5] But, at the first "summit" conference of the Allies, in December and January, General Arnold had taken his seat beside General Marshall, and

Admiral King, the Navy's Chief, as one of the three Joint Chiefs of Staff, who, with their three British counterparts, were to direct the Anglo-American war effort.

Meanwhile, General Arnold had been authorized to expand his force from 24 to 54 groups, then to 84, then to 115, and before 1942 was out, to 273 groups. One hundred and fifteen of these had to be ready by December 31, 1942; 224 by December 31, 1943.[6]

An expansion of one service in such proportions was without precedent in the history of war. Strongly backed by the President, the War Department provided the Army Air Forces with every possible advantage in carrying it out. Resources in money were now virtually unlimited. In competition with other arms for scarce resources the Air Forces were given the highest priorities, and were defended by the President in their claims on war production that conflicted with those of the Navy. They were allowed to recruit high-grade volunteers as pilots and ground technicians, outside of Selective Service, and given the privilege of creaming off the draftees who made the highest Army Classification scores. In 1943 they got 40 percent of Army recruits with the highest qualification ratings.[7]

1942–1944: a Hope Long Deferred

When Pearl Harbor plunged the United States into open war, the Air Forces' bombers were the only arm ready for early offensive action against Germany. To make such action effective at the earliest possible date the Army Air

Forces were authorized first call on the nation's resources for the build-up and training of a strategic air force.

Despite all these advantages favorable to the fulfillment of the most cherished dream of the American air leaders, not until the last months of 1944 did they get a chance to put to a full and fair test the decisiveness of independent air war.

In 1942, before American strategic bombers could get into action over Europe, the Royal Air Force was already heavily engaged in the strategic bombing of Germany. In May, General Harris's Bomber Command had been able to stage a 1000-bomber night raid on Cologne.

In March, when the War Department proposed its BOLERO-ROUNDUP plan, General Arnold backed it eagerly, although it gave his air force the secondary role of paving the way for a territorial invasion of the continent. He welcomed the plan because it enabled him to fight off the demands of naval and military commanders in other theaters for more and more planes, and get his heavy bombers concentrated in Europe. It gave him a chance to establish the basis for a strategic bombing force in England, and the Eighth Air Force was hastily assembled and trained, and its shipment begun.[8]

Then, in July, came Mr. Roosevelt's decision for TORCH which launched all the ready forces of the Allies into North Africa. TORCH drained off the strength of the new Eighth Air Force. It meant, as General Arnold put it, "dispersal of power even before we really had it." [9] All that the Eighth Air Force could do with its remnant of strength was to raid the submarine bases on the Brittany coast, and stage small practice raids on industrial targets in France.[10] On January 4, 1943, Mr. Churchill wrote in one of his "Minutes," "I note that the Americans have not yet succeeded in dropping a single bomb on Germany." [11]

But, later in January, at the Casablanca Conference, the Allied high command gave strategic bombing the top role in the Anglo-American offensive effort for 1943. Authorizing a Combined Bomber Offensive, they gave it, next to anti-submarine warfare, and aid to Russia, first claim on their combined resources. The Royal Air Force was to continue area bombing at night. The Eighth Air Force was to bomb selected industrial targets in daylight strikes. Germany was to be subjected to round-the-clock strategic bombing.

The kind of war the Army Air Forces so eagerly desired to wage had suddenly been given the green light. Before the end of the year they had two air forces, the Eighth under Maj. Gen. Ira C. Eaker, and the Fifteenth, under Maj. Gen. James H. Doolittle, fully engaged in strategic bombing, one based in England, the other in Italy, and between them capable of reaching targets all over Germany.

But 1943 was a year of bitter disappointments for the Army Air Forces. Their build-up fell short of their goals because of continued diversions of strength. At Casablanca the Americans had overcome the opposition of the British, led by Mr. Churchill, to the use of their heavy bombers for daylight precision bombing. They gained their point. But when their B–17's began to strike at sensitive targets inside Germany, the German defenses, not to mention the weather, rendered their bombing highly imprecise. What was worse, as soon as they got beyond the range of fighter escorts, the "Flying Fortresses" were found to be anything but invulnerable, or well enough armed to take care of themselves. The loss of bombers and crews shot down by German fighters mounted. Finally, in two great strikes on the German ball-bearing and aircraft industries at Schweinfurt and Regensburg, in August and October, while the bombing was effective, the rate of loss became intolerable. The American strategic forces had to be withdrawn from the air over Germany. As the British Air historians have said, it was all but a "tragic defeat." [12]

The Americans effected a phenomenal rally. They had at last been built up to full strength, and by a crash program, they had been provided with fighter escorts, first P–47 "Thunderbolts," and then P–51 "Mustangs" which, with droppable fuel tanks, could take the bombers all the way to their targets and tangle effectively with the fighter-planes of the *Luftwaffe*.[13]

But now the cross-Channel attack was less than six months away, and could not be launched unless the *Luftwaffe* was driven from the sky over France. And the Americans had learned that before they could bomb German targets effectively they would first have to cripple the German fighter force. This they did, single-handed, in a famous "Big Week," beginning February 23. But hardly was this done, and done in the nick of time, when both the British and the American strategic air forces came under the command of General Eisenhower, as Supreme Allied Commander, and were given as their primary mission the protection and support of the invasion of France.[14] The Army Air Forces had now amassed enough strength in Europe to perform this mission and at the same time to resume their pounding of strategic targets. But not until September, 1944, when the combined forces of the Allies had reached the borders of Germany, were they both fully equipped and free, at last, to demonstrate what independent war in the air could do.

The Army Air Forces, then, had only a little over six months in which to stage this demonstration: from September, 1944, through April, 1945, in Europe, and from November, 1944, through July, 1945, against Japan.

The reasons for this long postponement have become apparent in the foregoing narrative.

One was the stop-gap deployment of American forces in 1942. Both the War Department and the Navy had to disperse their forces all over the world to plug gaps in the defenses of the Allies. The Army Air Forces were the hardest hit since theirs was the ready power that could be most promptly applied at the danger-points. Their asset for which everybody now clamored was the key to their own program of strategy, the long-range bomber, which the War Department had only reluctantly let them have, and which as recently as 1938, at the demand of the Navy, it had forbidden them to fly more than a hundred miles offshore.[15] When the war struck the United States, the big bombers, as soon as they came out of the factories, were sent to defend the West Coast, and to hold the vital string of islands on the line between Hawaii and Australia; and presently were being flown or shipped to the Middle East, to shore up the embattled British, fighting off Rommel at the gate to Egypt and the Suez Canal. New output had to be shared with the Navy, rapidly developing its own fleet air arm, which included shore-based aircraft produced by the Army Air Forces.[16] During all this year of 1942, the Air Forces' production of planes was plagued by the lags in build-up from which the Army Air Forces, in spite of their privileges, suffered during the period of bottlenecks and shortages of critical facilities, lasting well into 1943, while the American war economy was getting into full production. In their sharp competition with the other services for top priorities they were supported by the War Department and strongly backed by the President, who declared the production of 82,000 combat aircraft in 1943 a "must," against the Navy's strenuous protests.[17] But their build-up to authorized strength was inevitably delayed.

The limitation on the development of an independent air strategy that was most persistent and serious, and the one to be emphasized here, was the grand strategy of the Allies, which required the use of air power for other strategic purposes than the direct bombardment of Germany: co-operation of land-based bombers with the Navy to quell the deadly U-boat menace in 1942 and 1943; [18] the protection and support of Allied forces in the Mediterranean, first in Tunisia, then in Sicily and Italy; and most important and demanding of all, the full use of air power to insure the success of OVERLORD, the great cross-Channel attack, in 1944.

The air leaders shared in all these decisions and supported them loyally. Some of the most respected and influential among them, British and American, including the American Air Chief, General Arnold and Lt. Gen. Carl Spaatz, who became Commanding General of the United States Strategic Air Forces in Europe, believed and argued that if the Allies concentrated their energies on strategic bombing they could soon bring Germany to unconditional surrender without an invasion. But this would have been a gamble on the untried. With large ground forces in hand, equipped, and approaching readiness, it was an unnecessary gamble, and it was not tried. The official Air historians of World War II are in agreement that the decision to subordinate strategic bombing to the demands of the great air-ground offensive of 1944 was correct and wise.

In the light of the foregoing survey two subjects call for special consideration. One is the co-operation of the Army Air Forces with the other services, since for three years they made their principal contributions to victory in co-operative combinations with them. The other is strategic bombardment, since this was a new kind of warfare.

Air Doctrines and Interservice Tension

Although the aspiration of the American air chiefs was to fight a war of their own, they did not question their obligation to perform the co-operative missions of an air force, both those which were traditional, and those required by emergencies that confronted the Allies with new situations.

They accepted these obligations, but they insisted on meeting them in their own way, in accordance with the doctrines of air war which they had developed in the interval between the first and second World Wars. The resultant system of doctrines may fairly be termed a military theology since it could not as yet be verified by experience.

At its core was the quite logical assumption that the range and speed which the airplane had acquired, com-

bined with the potential accuracy and destructiveness of
its impact, had introduced new dimensions of space, power,
and flexibility into air warfare which rendered obsolete
traditional ideas of co-operation with other forces.

Apart from the ambitions of the young American air
force to wage a war of its own, its doctrinal positions on co-
operation with forces of the other two older services sufficed
to get it embroiled in bitter struggles with both of them.
In 1942–43 it battled with the Army commanders over the
role and command of aviation in support of ground forces,
and during the same years it was engaged in a heated
struggle with the Navy over the command and employment
of shore-based bombers in the war to master the German
U-boats in the Atlantic. Both controversies were settled by
compromise, and on generally sounder lines, it would now
appear, than could have been foreseen. Both revolved
around the air forces' doctrine of command.

The Army Air Forces insisted that air forces must be
commanded and used only by air officers. Command of
specialized forces by branch-trained officers—an artillery
battalion by an Artillery officer, an engineer regiment by
an Engineer officer: this was nothing new. But those specialists took their orders from the commander of the
division, corps, or army to which they were assigned or
attached, almost always an Infantry general. What was
new and shocking was the high level of command at which
alone the new air leaders would consent to take orders.
They would recognize the right of a commander of another
service to give orders to an air force only if he was commander of a theater of operations, or a large task force.
Even then he could only assign the air commander a

mission required by the strategic plan, and he was not to decide how the air commander was to carry it out. In short, air was pulling out of its place in the integrated team of combined arms which the War Department had developed around divisions, corps, and armies.

To fleet commanders of the Navy and field commanders of the Army this was a shocking and dangerous doctrine. It struck explosively at the heart of two of their bred-in-the-bone convictions. One was that only a field general knew how to use an army, and only an old salt knew how to use a naval force. The other was that he could use his force effectively only if free to apply at ground and sea level the principle that command is one and indivisible.

No one was more inflexible in his convictions on this point than the Chief of Naval Operations and Commander-in-Chief of the U.S. Navy, Admiral Ernest J. King. Admiral "Ernie" King, whom Air Marshal Slessor has described as "that tough and unsentimental warrior," Professor Morison as "a man of adamant," was an air-minded admiral, but he set his face like flint against the doctrines and pretensions of the free-wheeling Army Air Forces.[19] He did not believe that the Army's big bombers could hit a target —a conviction confirmed by the useless performance of the B–17's in the critical battle of Midway in June, 1942— and he had no faith in strategic bombardment. To his own air arm he applied the doctrine of strict integration with surface forces under fleet command.[20]

This growing fleet air arm contained shore-based aircraft, including four-engine ("Liberator") bombers. But when Admiral Doenitz's U-boats began at once, in January, to butcher American shipping in sight of our Atlantic coast, the Navy, caught unprepared, had to call on the Army Air Forces for help. This was 1942, when General Arnold desperately needed every one of his bombers for the operational training of his crews and the build-up of the Eighth Air Force in England. To economize his bombers and to assure what he regarded as their effective use, he created an Army Air Forces Antisubmarine Command. It was presumably modelled on the famous British Coastal Command. This was under the general control of the British Admiralty.[21] But the U.S. Navy, disregarding Air doctrine, pressed its control of tactics and allocations of force down to the operational level.[22]

In the spring of 1942, General Sir John Dill, Chief of the British Mission in Washington, had said that he wasn't quite sure what his duties were, but "at least he provided neutral ground on which the American Army and Navy could meet." [23] Then in July, Admiral King made a move that raised interservice tension to a still higher pitch. The Combined Chiefs of Staff had committed a massive U.S. air force to the support of the SLEDGEHAMMER-ROUNDUP program of strategy, thereby nourishing the hope and ambition of the Army Air Forces to develop in the United Kingdom a force that they could get permission to use for the strategic bombardment of Germany. But in July, when TORCH was substituted for SLEDGEHAMMER, the Combined Chiefs declared that fifteen of the air groups earmarked for BOLERO, including three groups of heavy bombers, were now surplus to the requirements of a cross-Channel attack. Admiral King immediately began to urge that the fifteen groups be allocated to the Navy's war in the Pacific. General Arnold and the Air staff saw in this proposal a deadly threat to their dream of mounting a strategic air war in Europe.[24]

Admiral King was pressing hard on the young AAF's most sensitive nerve, and the two services moved toward a dangerous crisis in their internecine fight. General Arnold became convinced that Admiral King's object was to get control of his heavy bombing force.[25] A new crisis in the anti-submarine campaign brought the hostility between the two services to the point of outbreak. In the early spring of 1943, Admiral Doenitz, assembling his U-boats in wolf-packs, directed them with murderous success at the mid-Atlantic gap on the convoy line between England and America, where air escort cover from neither country could cover it. When Admiral King asked for more of the Air Forces' long-range bombers to cover the gap, General Arnold sent them to Newfoundland with instructions to the Air commander not to accept orders to cover convoys. This, the historian of the Navy has observed, "was the straw that broke the camel's back." [26] General Marshall, backed by Mr. Roosevelt, now stepped between the two mighty and incensed opposites and induced them to accept a truce. As soon as the two services could disentangle their forces, the Navy was to have undivided responsibility for the anti-submarine campaign. It was to be given 187 heavy bombers specially equipped for antisubmarine warfare by the Army Air Forces Antisubmarine Command, in exchange releasing the same number of its own "Liberators" to the Army Air Forces. And henceforth the Army Air Forces were to have undivided control of their own bombing forces.[27]

The Army Air and Ground Forces

The controversies of the American air chiefs with the old guard in the Army had a different history, if only because the American air force was still inside the War Department and subject to its ordinances.

In the new system of air doctrine the supreme goal and mission of air power was strategic bombing. Its missions in co-operation with land forces were redefined under three heads, in a fixed order of priority. The first was to cripple the enemy's air force and gain control of the air. The second was to isolate the battle area on a wide arc by bombing and strafing the enemy's approaches to it and the movement of his troops and supplies into it. The third was direct support on the field of battle. Only by strictly observing this order of priority could a modern air force realize the advantages of its mobility and speed, economize its power, and co-operate efficiently with army forces.

This concept of co-operation clashed with the War Department's traditional doctrine of air power. That doctrine gave the air arm the duty of holding an umbrella over each force of ground arms engaging the enemy, and of providing it with eyes that could see far ahead, and shoot out the eyes of the enemy. The new air force recognized these as its duties. But it proposed to raise its umbrella over the whole theater of operations, instead of providing one for each division, corps, or army. The speed and mobility of its planes would enable it to provide a local umbrella when necessary. The new air leaders put this duty of direct support lowest in their order of priorities. They regarded it as difficult, wasteful, and seldom likely to be necessary.[28]

Having failed to get independence, the Army Air Forces leaders got their doctrine of command recognized by the War Department in one of its Field Manuals, No. 31–35, issued in April, 1942.[29] But they were not satisfied because it provided that air force units might be assigned to the support of ground units, and that "the final decision as to priority of targets rested with the commander of the supported unit." Unfortunately, in order to protect the authority of the air commander, FM 31–35 made it all but impossible for air and ground forces to speak to each other in battle. It stationed with each large ground unit an air liaison officer. If the ground commander wanted air support he could request it only through this officer, who reported the request to the nearest airfield on a communications network of his own. By the time the air headquarters had decided whether or not to approve it, and, if it did, get bombers or fighters to the scene of action, they were often too late to be of any use.[30] And when they arrived the pilots were given no means of communicating with the force they were to support. The ground forces had to work up imperfect devices such as colored smoke puffs and cerise panels to signal to them.[31]

Lt. Gen. Lesley J. McNair, who became Commanding General of the Army Ground Forces in the War Department's reorganization in March, 1942, had been among the first to welcome the rising young air force to the American partnership of arms. But possessing an intelligence that, to an extraordinary degree, combined intellectual acumen and forward-looking open-mindedness with a sharp eye for the practical, he remained skeptical about the claims and doctrines of the air force chiefs until he could see these tested in practice. He at once laid himself out to provide such a test in his training program for 1942, believing it to be not only of vital importance in establishing sound doctrine, but equally important to success in accomplishing the huge task of giving the ground forces a realistic training for combat. Throughout 1942 he patiently tried to get air force units to train with his ground forces. In vain: the Army Air Forces did not provide them.[32] Desperately short of combat aircraft, they had the enormous task of training their own crews and they were straining every nerve to prepare for battle an effective strategic bombing force. Not only was this their main interest: it was what the strategy of 1942 and 1943 required. The result was that few divisions that went into battle even in 1944, had so much as seen American planes in the air, and had learned only in school how to make co-operation with them work.[33] The two services had become strangers to each other except at the top.

The American ground and air forces were plunged into battle in the Mediterranean in November, 1942, by the TORCH operation, with no practice in working together. The air generals, with an inadequate force hastily scrambled together, had all they could do in trying to overcome the air superiority of the *Luftwaffe*, and strike at the reinforcements that the Germans and Italians were pouring into Tunisia.[34] Ground commanders complained bitterly that they seldom saw an American plane. When they did their G.I.'s too often shot them down, and American airmen too

often bombed and strafed their brothers on the ground.[35]
Maj. Gen. Lloyd R. Fredendall, commanding the U.S. II
Corps, naturally tried to have protective air units attached
to his command under the permissive articles of FM 31–35.
Both parties, air and ground, became tense and dissatisfied.

An air umbrella, the bombing of targets in the battle
area, however desirable it might seem to ground forces in
action, was not the form of air support most closely related
to the mission of ground combat·forces. Aerial reconnaissance and observation, "eyes that could see far ahead":
this was the service of the airplane that had endeared it to
the Army in World War I. In World War II the performance of this function of support was sharply affected by the
new doctrines, interests, and organization of the air
forces.[36]

In 1941, the Army Air Forces was providing an "observation group"—a cluster of squadrons of various types—
which was allotted to each army corps and designed for
its use. But in 1943, pointing to the high mobility of
modern airplanes and invoking the doctrine of pooling and
flexibility, the Army Air Forces substituted for these
groups one reconnaissance squadron of high-speed fighter-
type planes for each corps and each armored division.
These squadrons were to perform the reconnaissance and
photo-mapping missions requested by ground commanders.
But they were wholly under air force control; their missions were subject to the air forces' doctrine of priorities;
and their equipment was designed primarily to meet the
air's own needs for reconnaissance. The large photo-maps
they produced did not contain the close-in, pinpoint information that ground commanders most needed; the

photographs were developed and interpreted by Air Intelligence officers at a distant base, and the intelligence was reported in terms from which it was difficult for ground officers to get the information they sought. In the Tunisian campaign the planes were equipped to take only oblique photographs, not the verticals that the ground forces required. Ground commanders complained that the intelligence disseminated to them not only did not meet their requirements, but was reaching them too late to be of use. In July, 1943, General McNair concluded, after studying the reports of the North African campaigns: "in general, our divisions and smaller units fought in North Africa with no air observation. Comparatively speaking, they attacked into the unknown although the need of air observation on close-in areas was ever-present."

The other service of air observation that was intimately and vitally important to ground combat forces was the spotting of artillery targets and the adjustment of artillery fires. Even before the war Army leaders had become anxious about the performance of this function to be expected from the high-speed reconnaissance planes that the Air Forces were developing for their own purposes, and were now exclusively producing. These fast planes could serve long-range corps and army artillery effectively, and they did; but they were useless for the artillery of shorter ranges on which divisions and regiments constantly and heavily depended to clear the way for their advance. In 1941, the Army Artillery Corps introduced into the gap a home-made expedient, which the Ground Forces adopted, and which solved the problem. This was the little unarmed two-seater Piper Cub, which an artillery officer could use as an airborne observation post. The Air Forces procured these inexpensive "grasshoppers" from the civilian manufacturer. The Army Artillery School trained the observers, and the Air Forces taught them to fly. Pairs of these little planes (known in the Army as "L–4's") were made organic in each artillery battalion and in each divisional and brigade artillery headquarters.

The ground Army had thus devised and acquired a miniature air force of its own. As soon as this attained the strength overseas, in the second half of 1943, to fully prove itself in combat, it achieved an immense popularity. The little "puddle-jumpers" (they were given many affectionate nicknames) could take off and land almost anywhere. They were always within reach; they could be used as the ground headquarters saw fit to use them; and their artillerymen pilots thoroughly understood the needs of the ground forces. They became a kind of mascot of the ground forces, as well as an indispensable military instrument.

From the first the Army Air Forces watched this development with a jealous eye, and repeatedly tried to bring it under their control. The War Department finally stipulated that they might be allowed to do so if the Army Ground Forces let its cub aviation expand beyond the original authorization. This threat created a sore spot in the relations between ground and air, and it became increasingly a source of irritation. For the ground forces in combat quickly found a variety of purposes for which their little "grasshoppers" could be employed—as "flying jeeps" for liaison between headquarters, for close-in photo-mapping, for night flying, for emergency re-supply, as flying ambulances, eventually even as carriers of rockets and light bombs; and they pressed not only for more of them but for improvements, and finally for an improved plane. But whenever General McNair recommended a change, watchful Air officers in the Pentagon would invoke the threat. The "light aviation" of the ground forces had to achieve its impressive success by ingenuity and enthusiasm, and making do with what it had.

Co-operation with Ground Forces, 1943–1945

In mid-1943, then, air-ground co-operation in the American forces in Europe presented an unhappy picture. By mid-1944 it had undergone a transfiguration. By March, 1945, in the judgment of General Eisenhower's Chief of Staff, Lt. Gen. Walter Bedell Smith, "the tactical coordination of air and ground forces has become an instrument of precision timing." [37]

The improvement can be attributed in part to the fact that by the summer of 1944, the Army Air Forces at last had ready forces in hand to perform a variety of tasks. Air spokesmen were prone to ascribe much of the credit for improvement to the victory of the air leaders in getting a satisfactory statement of their ambitions and doctrines written into the Bible of the Army when the War Department issued FM 100–20, *Command and Employment of Air Power*, on July 21, 1943, while the war between Air and Navy was at its height. This declared in capital letters (literally so) that "land power and air power are CO-EQUAL AND INTERINDEPENDENT FORCES: NEITHER IS AN AUXILIARY OF THE OTHER," and established the three missions of aviation co-operating with ground forces in the desired order of priority. The framers of this "declaration of independence," with characteristic respect for British precedents in their field, cited as firm ground for their position General Montgomery's "Notes on High Command in War," based on his experience in the triumphant sweep of the British Eighth Army from El Alamein to the Mareth Line. The historians of the Army Air Forces have followed them in ascribing much influence to General Montgomery's declaration in bringing Army commanders around to a more respectful view of air doctrines of co-operation with ground forces.[38]

The experience of both the British and American air forces in Africa certainly had much to do with the re-organizations of the air forces in the Mediterranean theater that took place in 1943.[39] They are too complicated to be followed here. The outcome important for our theme is that from them emerged, for use in Italy, a tactical air force, the Twelfth, alongside the Fifteenth Air Force, whose mission was strategic bombing. Tactical air forces were designed primarily to serve air force needs. But they brought together in a major command the commands, units, and types of aircraft most suitable for use in support of ground forces, and to be so used if not needed for missions of air warfare deemed more important at a given time; and this created a framework more favorable to air-ground collaboration.

But a historian trying to account for the improvements in collaboration which began to take place during the Italian campaign, and which had such happy consequences in northern Europe after D-Day in Normandy is not likely to rate too highly the influence of organizational changes and high-level definitions of doctrine. Too clearly the improvements that were essential grew up "in the field." They sprang from grass roots in the good will and efforts of air and ground officers who, in the bitter fighting of the Italian campaign, subordinated ambitions, doctrine, and prejudice to the task of finding practical solutions for the problems that confronted them in battle. They were officers of Lt. Gen. Mark W. Clark's Fifth Army and the tactical air command that was designated to work with it, Brig. Gen. Gordon P. Saville's XII Air Support Command.

The devices they worked out were simple and sensible. One was to locate side by side the Army Headquarters and that of the XII Air Support Command, so that the staffs and commanders were continuously aware of each others' plans and problems. Again, ground commanders were authorized to send liaison officers to airfields to explain the problems of their units, brief the pilots being sent to support them, and extract information about the situation ahead from air photographs which the air had taken for its own purposes. Finally, the air liaison officer with a ground force, now called a controller, or "Rover" control (variously nicknamed "Rover Joe," "Rover Pete," "Rover John," and the like), was authorized to ride forward in a jeep equipped with a high-frequency radio and talk the pilots on to profitable targets, or go up in a little artillery plane, dubbed a "Horsefly," and lead them in. Air and ground were at last authorized and equipped to talk to each other in battle.[40]

These arrangements did not revolutionize air-co-operation in Italy, but they worked so well that the OVERLORD planners studied them and wrote them, with further improvements, into the air plan for the cross-Channel invasion.[41] The Army Air Forces built up a great "tactical" air force, the Ninth, to co-operate with the American armies invading northern Europe and paired off one of its tactical air commands with each of the three U.S. armies. Even the strategic air forces were put at General Eisenhower's disposal to assist when needed, as at St. Lô on July 25, when they were brought thundering in over Normandy to blast a gap for the break-through of the U.S. First Army. Ground commanders ceased to complain and began to join in a rising chorus of praise.[42] On August 6 General Patton, as his Third Army raced to the Seine, was ready to entrust the safety of his open southern flank to the XIX Tactical Air Command. The most talked-about development during the break-out in August was the air-tank team in which an air controller sat with the commander of an armored squadron in the "point" tank, equipped with a VHF (very high frequency) radio, and exchanged requests, warnings, and intelligence with planes overhead detailed to provide the armored force with cover and "armed reconnaissance." [43] This was an exciting and spectacular war game. It was, of course, easier to team planes with fast-moving tank columns than with foot-slogging infantry, and the collaboration of air and tank crews was the outstanding success in air-ground co-operation in Europe.[44] But the two services were at last learning how to work together. The new practices would have worked sooner and better if the troops and pilots had been trained beforehand.[45] But the young Americans learned fast. Co-operation throve in a soil of daily association and mutual understanding. Air commanders, as well as the pilots put enthusiasm and energy into making the new arrangements work.[46] Maj. Gen. Elwood R. ("Pete") Quesada, commanding the tactical air command paired with Patton's Third Army, found himself embarrassed when General Bradley would thank him for fine support: "that was what we were there for," he said.[47] Of Quesada General Bradley wrote: he "had come into the war as a young and imaginative man unencumbered by the prejudices and theories of so many of his seniors on the employment of tactical air. To Quesada the fighter [plane] was a little-known weapon with vast unexplored possibilities in the support of ground troops." [48]

Meanwhile, in the Pacific highly effective co-operation between Army Air, the Army, and the Navy had been developing.[49] In the campaign to blot out the great naval and air base that the Japanese had fortified at Rabaul, air, naval, and amphibious land forces teamed up to strike with 1–2–3 punches as they climbed the ladder of the Solomon Islands from Guadalcanal. Land-based fighters and bombers of the Army Air Forces worked in partnership with Navy and Marine air in paralyzing Rabaul; Army bombers helped to keep it down once it had been isolated; and Army air performed both roles loyally and well in a theater, the South Pacific, in which the commander was an admiral.[50] In the Southwest Pacific Area, which was in effect an Army-directed theater, the strategic statesmanship of General MacArthur and the energy of his air commander, General George Kenney, combined to produce a most cordial and effective air-ground partnership. General MacArthur's strategy was to use land-based planes to cover his leaps up the north coast of New Guinea and into the Philippines. This required little close-in support. Each of the partners, ground and air, got what it wanted most. The Army had its leaps covered and extended. The Army Air Forces got island bases from which to achieve air supremacy, and advance rapidly toward points where its bombers might get at Japan.

The Big Bomber Offensives, 1944–1945

We left the strategic bombing of Germany in the spring of 1944 when the U.S. strategic bombing force had, in the nick of time, scotched the fighters of the *Luftwaffe*. Although they then almost immediately came under General Eisenhower's command, they now had the strength to continue the bombing of Germany as well as support the invasion, and the American and British heavy bombing forces began to strike hard at the German synthetic oil industry.[51]

The two strategic forces, the British by night and the American by day, had for over two years been pounding Germany with increasing mass, continuity, and violence. They had blasted and burned great cities, as the British Bomber Command did Hamburg, with its fearful fire-storm raid, as early as July, 1943. Their bombs had wrecked the buildings housing the production of vital necessities for the waging of war, as the Americans had in their costly attacks on the ball-bearing and aircraft factories at Schweinfurt and Regensburg, in August and October, 1943.

Yet when the United States Strategic Bombing Survey made its searching study in 1945, it was found that before the summer of 1944, this huge effort had produced far less effect than had been supposed.

Prior to the summer of 1943 it had had "no appreciable effect" either on munitions output or on the national economy in general." Until July, 1944, the total armaments production of Germany steadily increased.[52] The monthly production of aircraft as late as September, 1944, was over 4,000 planes, a figure to which it had leaped from 2,445 in January.[53] Bombing slowed down the expansion of output—in the first quarter of 1944 by as much as 10 percent. The Survey concluded that in 1943, it inflicted a total loss of output that amounted to not more than 3 to 5 percent.[54] Not until the bombing forces launched their systematic bombing of oil production after D-Day, and their transportation campaign beginning in September, did they inflict wounds that proved to be mortal.[55] Nor did the civilian morale of the Germans crack under the bombing of their cities, although 305,000 civilians were killed, 780,000 were wounded, and 5,000,000 had to be evacuated.[56] The government managed to keep the standard of living of the survivors virtually unimpaired until late in 1944, and the Germans took bombing as stoically as had the British in 1940 and 1941. One is reminded of George Meredith's description of storm waves breaking on an ocean beach:

Thundering like ramping hosts of warrior horse
To throw that faint thin line upon the shore.

If the unhinging of the German economy was so long delayed, this was not because the blows delivered from the air had not been increasingly devastating and accurate,[57] but because the whole program of strategic bombing had been based on a mistaken conception of the German war economy. Unlike those of England and the United States it had not, until 1943, been systematically mobilized for war. The Germans were later found to have had reserves of machine-tools, and raw materials which sufficed to the very end for the manufacture of guns, ammunition, military vehicles, aircraft, and engines, and they had enough resources of motive power (except toward the last, fuel oil), to propel their aircraft and other military machines and keep their factories running. When a war industry was hit, they had enough unused factory space and manpower to effect its dispersal. They never fully mobilized their reserve of manpower. Women were not mobilized, as in England and the United States. Even when the driving genius of Speer rationalized and stepped up war production in 1943–44, he rarely put its factories on a double shift.[58] Yet the output steadily increased.

But the Strategic Bombing Survey left no doubt that the independent air war which the Royal Air Force and the United States Strategic Bombing Forces were finally able to mount from September, 1944, until April, 1945, when they ran out of targets, unhinged and paralyzed its capacity to make war.[59] They achieved this effect by a more fortunate choice of targets and by the sheer weight of their assault, rather than by precision bombing.

The strategic air forces were far from being the instrument of precision they were originally intended to be.

In 1941, the British had given up precision bombing in daylight as hopeless and went over to area bombing at night.[60] The young American air force had been confident that, with its Norden bombsight and its rugged B–17's, it could make selective bombing a decisive success. It "hung up its hat" on the policy of precision bombing in daylight.[61]

Having gone over to night bombing, in 1941, the Royal Air Force again met with a costly and bitter disappointment. Their bombers could not cope with the antiaircraft fire and dazzling searchlights in the smoke and haze over German cities; often they could not even find the cities they were to bomb.[62] Then, in 1942, General Sir Arthur Harris, put in command of the British Bomber Command transfigured it into a formidably effective force. He did not approach area bombing as a necessity: he embraced it as an ideal. He openly scorned the advocates of selective bombing as peddlers of "panaceas." At the same time he developed techniques for making his area bombing effective: radio directional beaming; radar aiming; and Pathfinder forces which lighted up target cities with flares and incendiaries. In January, 1943, when Churchill tried at Casablanca to shake the faith of the inexperienced Americans in precision bombing of "target systems," and get them to join the British Bomber Command in a conclusive campaign of night attacks on German morale—a genuine "Combined Bomber Offensive"—he could point to an impressive record: Harris's "1,000-bomber" raids, beginning with Cologne in May, had got well along with the destruction of German cities.[63]

The Americans stood their ground and each force was

allowed to go its own way. Daylight bombing, in 1943, brought the American strategic air force to the brink of disaster. But when the U.S. Strategic Air Forces, equipped with fighter escorts, resumed its offensive in the spring of 1944, their commander, Lt. Gen. Carl Spaatz, stuck to the American goal of bringing the Germans to surrender by selective bombing of vital "target systems" in daylight. The Americans not only believed it to be more effective: they were opposed to the mass bombing of civilians.[64] In January, General Eaker, supporting Spaatz in opposing it, wrote: ". . . . you and Bob Lovett are right and we should never allow the history of this war to convict us of bombing the man in the streets." [65] Nevertheless the "spillage" of badly aimed bombs wrought havoc and destruction in the residential areas of cities in or near which "military" targets were located. And to overcome the interruptions imposed on their offensive by the weather over Europe the Americans adopted the techniques of the Royal Air Force for bombing through overcast.[66] This was blind bombing and hardly less indiscriminate than area bombing at night.

In the final period of the war the line between selective bombing and area bombing all but disappeared. On the one hand, General Harris was ordered, against his will, to join in the bombing of oil and transportation targets which his force was now equipped and trained to do effectively.[67] On the other, the American commanders, in spite of their reluctance, had been directed to engage in massive attacks on cities. In January, 1945, the Allied air leaders, meeting with the Combined Chiefs of Staff at Malta, obtained their authorization to direct a series of such attacks on Berlin and cities in east-central Germany not previously bombed. General Marshall supported the proposal, and General Arnold, although he had repeatedly expressed his opposition to morale bombing, gave his consent. The military purpose of these attacks was to help the Russians by hampering the movement of German reinforcements to the Eastern Front, but they were also intended to increase the confusion and panic in these cities frightened by the advance of the Soviet armies and crowded with refugees.[68] The Americans smashed at Berlin on February 3 with about a thousand "heavies," killing some 25,000 people, and on February 26, and again on March 18, with even more massive and devastating blows.[69] Meanwhile, on the night of February 13–14 the British hit Dresden, where the streets were crowded with civilian evacuees fleeing before the advancing Soviet army. The next morning, while the smoke from the fires kindled by the British was still rising 15,000 feet into the air over the mangled city, the Americans struck at it with another smashing raid.[70] In their directives for these attacks the American commanders listed specific military targets. They were nevertheless terror raids. The moral of Tolstoi's *War and Peace* was receiving a fresh illustration. The grim logic of war had taken it out of the hands of the men charged with its direction.

Strategic Co-operation

As we have seen, much, indeed most, of the effort expended by the Army Air Forces in World War II was devoted to operations in various combinations with land and sea forces. Ironically, much of the most effective work in the strategic bombing of Germany was done while the air forces were co-operating with the ground forces.[71] They learned the efficacy of transportation bombing when they reluctantly accepted, under General Eisenhower's orders, the mission of bombing the French transportation system to pave the way for the cross-Channel attack.[72] It was the swift advance of the armies across France and into the Low Countries that wrecked the radio air-warning net by which the enemy had directed his fighters against the streams of bombers en route to targets in Germany, and thereby made possible the deadly effectiveness of the final bombing assaults. Again, the air attacks on the German transportation network and on the cities of the Ruhr in March, 1945, which, in the findings of the Strategic Bombing Survey, ranked with the attacks on oil in unhinging the German war economy, were both made at the request of General Eisenhower, to speed the advance of his armies into Germany.[73] And it is to be remembered that when the Allied strategic air forces dealt the coup de grâce to Germany's economy and morale, the Soviet and Allied ground forces had shut the Germans up into their homeland and were striking from the East into its vitals. Whatever might have been, the utter defeat of Germany in April, 1945, was a victory of combined arms.

Against Japan the Army Air Forces launched its strategic air war in November, 1944, from the Marianas, which Admiral Nimitz's fleet and ground forces had captured the preceding March. It was carried out by the XXI Bomber Command, armed with B–29 superbombers, and commanded in the decisive stage of its campaign by a tough and ruthlessly logical young air general, Curtis LeMay, who is now Chief of the Air Force.[74] The XXI Bomber Command was part of the Twentieth Air Force. This was placed directly under General Arnold and the Joint Chiefs of Staff and was therefore not under the control of the Pacific theater headquarters.[75]

Until March, 1945, General LeMay continued a campaign of high-level strikes at selected targets in the Japanese war economy which his predecessor had initiated. It was a failure. Japanese fighters over the targets were effective; bombing was inaccurate, and losses in B–29's and their precious crews mounted.[76] In March, he decided on a new plan. This was to send his superbombers in at a low level, armed with napalm fire-bombs, over the flimsy cities of Japan, by night, and burn them out. The crews were instructed how to locate the most crowded and inflammable residential quarters.[77]

General LeMay notified General Arnold of his plan only on the day before he put it into effect, on the night of March 9–10.[78] He dealt his first blow at Tokyo. It was frightfully successful. 83,793 men, women, and children were reduced to "a midden of smoking flesh"; 40,918 were injured; 1,008,005 people were rendered homeless. More than fifteen square miles of the city were burnt out. The heat of the fire-storms ignited brought the water in the canals of the city to a boil. Only fifteen B–29's were lost in the raid.[79]

With the help of the Washington Air headquarters staff General LeMay now marked thirty-three urban areas for destruction.[80] In all sixty-six Japanese cities were subjected to fire blitzes; 330,000 civilians were killed and 8,500,000 had their homes destroyed.[81] Most of this damage was done before he was directed to drop the two atomic bombs, on Hiroshima and Nagasaki, on August 6. The air campaign was so overwhelmingly devastating that, in the opinion of the Strategic Bombing Survey, it would have brought surrender within a few more months even if the atomic bombs had not been dropped.[82] General LeMay could be satisfied that he had shown what independent air war can do.[83]

But the strategic bombing of Japan became effective only after sea-air-ground offensives had brought the B–29's within range of its home-islands, shorn away its new empire, and defeated its Navy and air force; and only after submarines and the naval blockade had strangled its shipping and war economy.[84]

Retrospect

The defeat, then, both of Germany and Japan, was inflicted by a combined team of Allied ground-sea-and-air forces.

In Europe Allied strategy centered on invasion by a force of combined arms. In the post-invasion phase ground operations were as decisive as air operations in pushing Germany to the brink of disaster. What can fairly be said of the decisiveness of strategic bombing in Europe is that it hastened the internal collapse of Germany, though this had not had time to produce a decisive effect on the German ground combat forces when the Nazi Government surrendered.[85]

In the Pacific war the U.S. Navy and the Army Air Forces, in combination, struck at the Japanese with such conclusive effect that an invasion was unnecessary. This was an achievement unprecedented in the history of war. But the dream and ultimate goal of air war is to produce surrender by air power with only incidental help from other forces.[86] In 1945, this dream did not come true. Furthermore, strategic bombing both in Germany and against Japan had proved to be a bludgeon, producing its effect by cumulative weight and mass laceration, rather than by a surgical operation, as its original advocates had hoped.

Strategic air war as the offensive par excellence had been the inspiration and goal of the pioneers and leaders of air power, British and American, and as such had shaped the mighty force the Americans created and their doctrines for its employment. The United States strategic air forces were a costly instrument of warfare in money, skills, and scarce resources, if not in men. In the short time at the end of the war, when these forces could be used with relative independence, strategic bombing developed a terrifying capacity for unselective destructiveness. It had not proved its decisiveness except in hastening the end and, incidentally, in providing a carrier for the first atomic bombs. Certainly, the sea-and-air power that had enringed and blockaded Nazi Europe and far-off Japan and made them accessible to assault from sea, ground, and air; certainly, the advance of air-assisted ground armies converging until they met in the heart of the Reich and at the gates of Japan, had been equally "decisive." What is incontestable is that the ways in which air power was used by the Americans and the British in World War II had a decisive effect on its course and outcome and irreversible consequences for the future of warfare and of strategy.

NOTES

INTRODUCTION

1. The major official works of reference are: Mark S. Watson, *Chief of Staff: Prewar Plans and Preparations* (Washington, D.C., 1950); Ray S. Cline, *Washington Command Post: The Operations Division* (Washington, D.C., 1951); Maurice Matloff and Edwin S. Snell, *Strategic Planning for Coalition Warfare, 1941-1942* (Washington, D.C., 1953); Maurice Matloff, *Strategic Planning for Coalition Warfare, 1943-1944* (Washington, D.C., 1959); and Richard M. Leighton and Robert W. Coakley, *Global Logistics and Strategy, 1940-1943* (Washington, D.C., 1955)—all in *U.S. Army in World War II*, ed. K. R. Greenfield (Washington, D.C.: Office of the Chief of Military History, Department of the Army). *Grand Strategy, 1939-1945*, Vols. I, II, V, VI of a six volume series published to date, in *History of the Second World War*, United Kingdom Military Series, ed. J. R. M. Butler (London: Her Majesty's Stationery Office). For a synthesis of the diplomatic aspects of the war brought up to date: John L. Snell, *Illusion and Necessity: The Diplomacy of Global War* (Boston: Houghton Mifflin Co.), scheduled for publication in the fall of 1963, which I have read in manuscript. (Footnotes in succeeding chapters often refer to the above-cited works.)

CHAPTER I

1. William L. Langer and S. Everett Gleason, *The Undeclared War* (New York: Harper & Bros., 1953).

2. The President declared that the defense of the Western Hemisphere would be the aim of the military policy of the United States on November 14, 1938, six weeks after Munich. Stetson Conn and Byron S. Fairchild, *The Framework of Hemisphere Defense* (Washington, D.C., 1960, in *U.S. Army in World War II*), pp. 3–5. The "Rainbow" plans, evolved by the Joint Board in 1939–41, contemplated offensive action by the United States if it became involved in the war in alliance with Great Britain. Watson, *Chief of Staff*, pp. 103–4; Matloff and Snell, *Strategic Planning*,

1941-1942, pp. 32–46. The mobilization plans of the War Department called for an expansion and training of its forces to meet the contingency of having to send the Army overseas as in World War I.

3. In their secret "ABC" conferences with representatives of the British military staff in January–March, 1941. Matloff and Snell, *Strategic Planning, 1941-1942*, pp. 25–48; Watson, *Chief of Staff*, pp. 367–82.

4. For the planning and execution of TORCH, George F. Howe, *Northwest Africa: Seizing the Initiative in the West* (Washington, D.C., 1957, in *U.S. Army in World War II*).

5. Maurice Matloff, "The 90-Division Gamble," in *Command Decisions*, ed. K. R. Greenfield (Washington, D.C.: Department of the Army, 1960), pp. 365–81; Robert R. Palmer, "Mobilization of the Ground Army," in *Organization of Ground Combat Troops* (Washington, D.C., 1947, in *U.S. Army in World War II*), pp. 225–30.

6. The date of the JCS directive was 2 July 1942. The strategic plan is described in John Miller, jr., *Guadalcanal: The First Offensive* (Washington, D.C., 1949, in *U.S. Army in World War II*).

7. By 3 December 1942, seventeen U.S. Army divisions and 66 combat air groups were overseas. Not to mention the two Marine divisions then in the Pacific and engaged on Guadalcanal, nine Army divisions and "about one-third of the Army's air combat groups" were deployed against Japan. The total of Army forces, ground and air, thus deployed (461,000) exceeded by about 50,000 those deployed against Germany (411,000). Matloff and Snell, *Strategic Planning, 1941-1942*, p. 359.

8. Matloff, *Strategic Planning, 1943-1944*, pp. 230–35.

9. In *U.S. Army in World War II* the fullest account is in G. A. Harrison, *Cross-Channel Attack* (Washington, D.C., 1951).

10. The evolution of the plan is traced by Matloff. Its military aspects are reviewed and summed up by Louis Morton, "The Decision to Drop the Atomic Bomb," *Foreign Affairs*, XXV, No. 2 (Jan., 1957), pp. 334–53. Its diplomatic and political aspects are conveniently and critically reviewed in John L. Snell's forthcoming *Illusion and Necessity: The Diplomacy of Global War, 1939-1945*.

11. Louis Morton, "Soviet Intervention in the War with Japan," *Foreign Affairs*, XL, No. 4 (July, 1962), pp. 653–62—an authoritative review of the reasons why we wanted the U.S.S.R. to enter the war against Japan.

12. Matloff and Snell, *Strategic Planning, 1941-1942*, pp. 46, 80–81.

13. Louis Morton, "National Policy and Military Strategy," *Virginia Quarterly Review*, XXXVI, No. 1 (Winter, 1960), pp. 7–10.

14. K. R. Greenfield, "Coalition Strategy: the Army's Outlook," *The Historian and the Army* (New Brunswick: Rutgers University Press, 1954), pp. 28–59.

15. It is necessary to say: "in general," because of the sharp divergence of opinion that arose in 1944 over the advisability of starving the Italian campaign to invade Southern France. See below, pp. 40–41.

16. John Ehrman defines Mr. Churchill's interest in a more active intervention in the Balkans in *Grand Strategy*, Vol. V, pp. 95, 111–13; and presents the evidence in Appendix VI, pp. 554–56. Herbert Feis reviews

the evidence in *Churchill, Roosevelt, and Stalin* (Princeton: Princeton University Press, 1957), pp. 344ff.

17. Matloff, *Strategic Planning, 1943-1944*, pp. 469-72. General Mark Clark states his view that this strategy would have been desirable for military and political reasons in *Calculated Risk* (London: Harrap & Co., 1951), pp. 347-52.

18. According to Averell Harriman's and General Deane's reports from Moscow. Matloff, *Strategic Planning, 1943-1944*, pp. 302-6.

19. Herbert Feis weighs this proposal of Stalin to Churchill in *Churchill, Roosevelt, and Stalin*, pp. 444-45.

20. *Ibid.*, pp. 338-43, 447-53. In November, 1943, en route to Tehran he had said to his military chiefs: "We should not get roped into accepting any European sphere of influence." Matloff, *Strategic Planning, 1943-1944*, p. 342.

21. Harry S Truman, *Memoirs*, Vol. I: *A Year of Decisions* (New York: Doubleday & Co., 1955), pp. 211-17; Winston S. Churchill, *Triumph and Tragedy* (Boston: Houghton Mifflin Co., 1953), pp. 501ff.; Feis, *Churchill, Roosevelt, and Stalin*, pp. 596-612.

22. Forrest C. Pogue, *The Supreme Command* (Washington, D.C., 1954, in *U.S. Army in World War II*), p. 468.

23. Matloff, *Strategic Planning, 1943-1944*, p. 533.

24. Ehrman, *Grand Strategy*, V, pp. 25-48.

25. Morton, "Soviet Intervention," *Foreign Affairs*, XL, pp. 653-62. For General MacArthur's advocacy of Soviet intervention, p. 658.

CHAPTER II

1. "OVERLORD versus the Mediterranean at the Cairo-Tehran Conferences," *Command Decisions*, pp. 255-85; "OVERLORD Revisited: an Interpretation of American Strategy in Europe in World War II," *American Historical Review* (July, 1963), pp. 919-37.

2. Matloff and Snell, *Strategic Planning, 1941-1942*, pp. 185-86, 193. A full account of the plan and its evolution is given in Harrison, *Cross-Channel Attack*, Chaps. I-III and V.

3. Matloff and Snell, *Strategic Planning, 1941-1942*, pp. 186, 241-42.

4. Quoted in *ibid.*, p. 156. See also p. 190.

5. Robert E. Sherwood, *Roosevelt and Hopkins: An Intimate History* (New York: Harper & Bros., 1948), p. 594.

6. Captain Harry C. Butcher, *My Three Years with Eisenhower* (New York: Simon & Schuster, 1946), p. 29. Butcher quotes him further as saying: "I'm right back to December 15th."

7. Letter to the President, 10 August 1943, in Henry L. Stimson and McGeorge Bundy, *On Active Service in Peace and War* (New York: Harper & Bros., 1947), p. 437.

8. At Casablanca the Joint Chiefs of Staff informed the British of

their intention to press their advantage against the Japanese. The British acquiesced, not without argument, but without formal protest. Matloff, *Strategic Planning, 1943–1944*, pp. 135–39. At TRIDENT the JCS obtained a ratification of their plans for Pacific offensives from the Combined Chiefs. *Ibid.*, p. 138.

9. *Ibid.*, p. 106.

10. Beginning at Casablanca, where General Sir Alan Brooke, Chairman of the British Chiefs of Staff, assured the Americans that "we would definitely count on re-entering the Continent in 1944 on a large scale." *Ibid.*, p. 27.

11. Leighton, "OVERLORD Revisited," p. 936. It can be argued that this point had been passed at QUADRANT. The qualified decision reached at Quebec "set in motion plans and preparations that acquired a momentum that with the mere passage of time became increasingly difficult to reverse." Harrison, *Cross-Channel Attack*, p. 100.

12. Ehrman, *Grand Strategy*, V, p. 361.

13. Matloff, *Strategic Planning, 1943–1944*, p. 132 says 26 to 30. More would be coming in. Only 29 would be fully equipped.

14. *Ibid.*, p. 133.

15. "The Navy's 1944 shipbuilding program called for a 50 percent increase over the previous year." Harrison, *Cross-Channel Attack*, p. 104.

16. En route to the TRIDENT Conference on board the "Queen Mary," General Alan Brooke made the following entries in his diary:

7 May: "There is no doubt that, unless the Americans are prepared to withdraw more shipping from the Pacific, our strategy in Europe will be drastically affected. Up to the present the bulk of the American Navy is in the Pacific and larger land and air forces have gone to that theatre than to Europe in spite of all that we have said about the necessity of beating Germany first."

10 May: "I do not look forward to these meetings: in fact I hate the thought of them. They will entail hours of argument and hard work trying to convince them that Germany must be defeated first. . . . It is all so maddening." Quoted in Arthur Bryant, *The Turn of the Tide* (New York: Doubleday & Co., 1957), pp. 497 and 500.

17. For an account of its origins, evolution, and achievements, Harrison, *Cross-Channel Attack*, pp. 47–82.

18. But largely armored amtracks (LVT's) and small tank-landing vessels (LCT–7's) at the expense of LST's. Leighton, "OVERLORD versus the Mediterranean," *Command Decisions*, p. 261.

19. Actually not all of this output, since six of the LST's produced were reserved by the Navy for conversion into amphibious repair ships to be used in the Pacific. Leighton, letter to the author, 20 February 1962, based on the MS of Global Logistics and Strategy, 1944–1945.

20. Allocation of American resources to the Pacific was determined exclusively by the American Joint Chiefs, notwithstanding the principle of pooled Anglo-American resources. At Cairo and after, when the Allies were wrestling with the intricate and thorny problem of finding enough

LST's for OVERLORD, "the British felt uneasily that they might not be able, in this critical case, to scrutinize the problem as a whole," a method the combined planners had found effective in solving other world-wide problems confronting the Combined Chiefs. Ehrman, *Grand Strategy*, V, pp. 37–38.

21. "By D-day over a million and a half American troops were in the United Kingdom poised for the attack." Matloff, *Strategic Planning, 1943–1944*, p. 408. For the CCS directive to General Eisenhower as Supreme Allied Commander, Pogue, *Supreme Command*, pp. 53–55.

22. Charles P. Stacey, *The Canadian Army, 1939–1945: an Official Historical Summary* (Ottawa: King's Printer, 1948), pp. 83–86.

23. "The whole frame of British field command was established in the spring and early summer [of 1943]." By July their 21 Army Group, Second British Army, and the First Canadian Army "all had functioning headquarters." Until October the U.S. V Corps was the highest American tactical headquarters in the United Kingdom. The War Department provided no Table of Organization for the American officers of COSSAC's staff. They functioned on detached service from the Plans Section of ETOUSA. When in October the United States activated an army group and the First U.S. Army, General Bradley doubled in brass as Commanding General of both. Harrison, *Cross-Channel Attack*, pp. 52–53.

24. Matloff, *Strategic Planning, 1943–1944*, p. 23.

25. Dwight D. Eisenhower, *Crusade in Europe* (New York: Doubleday & Co., 1952), p. 221; Sherwood, *Roosevelt and Hopkins*, p. 591.

26. Ehrman, *Grand Strategy*, V, pp. 43–48.

27. Winston S. Churchill, *The Hinge of Fate* (Boston: Houghton Mifflin Co., 1950), p. 346.

28. Gordon A. Harrison, Operation OVERLORD, an unpublished address delivered at the Army War College, 19 November 1951, quoted in Greenfield, *Historian and the Army*, p. 52.

29. The quotations are from Greenfield, *ibid.*, pp. 58–59.

CHAPTER III

1. Sherwood, *Roosevelt and Hopkins*, p. 446.

2. Ehrman, *Grand Strategy*, VI, p. 343.

3. Harrison, *Cross-Channel Attack*, p. 92.

4. Bryant, *Turn of the Tide*, p. 335.

5. William D. Leahy, *I Was There* (New York: McGraw Hill, 1950), pp. 103, 106.

6. William R. Emerson, "F.D.R. (1941–1945)," in *The Ultimate Decision: the President as Commander-in-Chief*, ed. Ernest R. May (New York: Braziller, 1960), p. 144 and *passim*.

7. Tabulated in Appendix to this chapter, pp. 80–84.

8. Emerson, "F.D.R.," pp. 135–36. For the order placing the Office of Emergency Management in the Executive Office of the President, R. Elber-

ton Smith, *The Army and Economic Mobilization* (Washington, D.C., 1958, in *U.S. Army in World War II*), pp. 100–1.

9. Stimson and Bundy, *On Active Service*, pp. 413–15.

10. Watson, *Chief of Staff*, pp. 5–7, 127–31; Emerson, "F.D.R.," pp. 139–42; *Army Air Forces in World War II* (hereafter referred to as *AAF History*) eds. W. F. Craven and James L. Cate (Chicago: University of Chicago Press, 1948–1955), Vol. I, *Early Plans and Preparations*, pp. 101–4, 107; Vol. VI, *Men and Planes*, pp. 264–65. When Marshall raised the question whether the President meant one-half of the planes scheduled for delivery or those actually delivered, F.D.R. said "breezily": "Don't let me see that chart again . . ." Watson, *ibid.*, p. 308.

11. Matloff and Snell, *Strategic Planning, 1941–1942*, pp. 12ff, 19ff; Emerson, "F.D.R.," p. 144ff.

12. Soviet Union: Maurice Matloff, "Franklin Delano Roosevelt as War Leader," *Total War and Cold War*, ed. Harry L. Coles (Columbus: Ohio State University Press, 1962), p. 46. China: Matloff and Snell, *Strategic Planning, 1941–1942*, pp. 73–75.

13. Matloff and Snell, *ibid.*, pp. 64–65, 69–70, 78.

14. In April 1941 President Roosevelt had called General Embick back to Washington to advise him on strategy. *Ibid.*, p. 50. Before going to the White House with General Embick, General Marshall said to his plans staff on April 16: [we must] "begin the education of the President as to the true strategic situation—this coming after a period of being influenced by the State Department. . . . We must tell him what he has to work with." The President nevertheless decided to send additional Army forces overseas. (The Germans had, meanwhile, in June, attacked Russia.) *Ibid.*, pp. 51–53.

15. Emerson, "F.D.R.," pp. 144–45. In corroboration see Watson, *Chief of Staff*, pp. 132–33.

16. Matloff and Snell, *Strategic Planning, 1941–1942*, pp. 28–29 for Mr. Roosevelt's decisive intervention in defining the bases for the first Anglo-American staff conversations ("ABC") in Jan.–Feb. 1941.

17. *Ibid.*, p. 46; Matloff, in Coles, *Total War*, pp. 48–49.

18. Watson, *Chief of Staff*, pp. 331–66; Matloff and Snell, *Strategic Planning, 1941–1942*, pp. 58–62; Smith, *Economic Mobilization*, p. 135; Leighton and Coakley, *Global Logistics*, pp. 126–37.

19. For Churchill: Ehrman, *Grand Strategy*, VI: *October 1944–August 1945*, pp. 315ff. For Roosevelt: *ibid.*, pp. 339–45; Emerson, "F.D.R.," pp. 174–75.

20. Ehrman, *Grand Strategy*, VI, p. 344. In the spring of 1942 Arnold and Marshall asked the Combined Chiefs to cut the allotment of airplanes to the Soviet Union, but dropped the proposal as useless "since Mr. Hopkins as an individual will get the President to overrule any such decision of the Combined Chiefs of Staff." Matloff and Snell, *Strategic Planning, 1941–1942*, p. 208. See also Emerson, "F.D.R.," p. 167, based on a study by Captain Tracey Kittredge for the Joint Chiefs of Staff Historical Section (in MS).

21. Emerson, "F.D.R.," p. 172, who does not mention the exception.

22. Ehrman, *Grand Strategy*, VI, p. 344.

23. For Mr. Roosevelt's reversal of the American position on the ROUNDUP-

BOLERO plan, Sherwood, *Roosevelt and Hopkins*, pp. 600–12, 615; Harrison, *Cross-Channel Attack*, pp. 26–32; Matloff and Snell, *Strategic Planning, 1941–1942*, pp. 266–84; Emerson, "F.D.R.," pp. 155–58.

24. For his alterations of the draft instructions submitted by the War Department, Sherwood, *ibid.*, pp. 602–6; Matloff and Snell, *ibid.*, pp. 273–84 and Appendix B; Emerson, *ibid.*, pp. 156–57.

25. Harrison, *Cross-Channel Attack*, p. 11; Matloff and Snell, *ibid.*, p. 105. He left Churchill in no doubt where his main interest lay. On March 9 he cabled him: "I am becoming more and more interested in the establishment of a new front this summer." Hopkins was pressing this on him. In a memo for F.D.R. on March 14 he wrote: "I doubt if anything is as important as getting some sort of front this summer against Germany." Sherwood, *ibid.*, pp. 518–19.

26. Stimson and Bundy, *On Active Service*, p. 425.

27. Matloff, *Strategic Planning, 1943–1944*, pp. 124–25.

28. Richard M. Leighton, "U.S. Merchant Shipping and the British Import Crisis," in *Command Decisions*, pp. 199–223.

29. "under bare-boat charter for the duration of the war." *Ibid.*, p. 222.

30. For JCS preparations to meet the British at TRIDENT, Cline, *Washington Command Post*, pp. 219–20.

31. Leahy, *I Was There*, p. 156. Mr. Roosevelt's copy of their briefing paper, bearing his annotations in pencil, is in the Franklin D. Roosevelt Library at Hyde Park, N.Y.

32. For the "feasibility dispute" and its military consequences, Civilian Production Administration, *Industrial Mobilization for War* (Washington, D.C., 1947), pp. 282–92; Smith, *Economic Mobilization*, pp. 154–58; Leighton and Coakley, *Global Logistics*, pp. 602–9, 633.

33. For the official historian's account of TRIDENT, Matloff, *Strategic Planning, 1943–1944*, pp. 126–35. Dr. Richard M. Leighton, also an official historian of the Army, was the first to call attention to the President's move at the first session of the conference (in his paper "OVERLORD Revisited," December, 1961), noting the discrepancy between Dr. Matloff's conclusions and the facts that he presents. Professor Emerson, though following Dr. Matloff's account, failed to note that the President took his own line at TRIDENT. He nevertheless concludes that prior to the Quebec Conference (QUADRANT) in August, 1943, as well as thereafter, "basic decisions that molded strategy were made by the Commander-in-Chief himself, against the advice of his own chiefs and in concert with Mr. Churchill and the British Chiefs." Emerson, "F.D.R.," pp. 154–55.

34. Matloff, *Strategic Planning, 1943–1944*, pp. 347–52, 360, 369–73; Richard M. Leighton, "OVERLORD versus the Mediterranean at the Cairo-Tehran Conferences," *Command Decisions*, pp. 266–71, 278–82.

35. Emerson, "F.D.R.," pp. 160, 163; and letter to the author, 21 January 1961. "This broken promise to China . . . greatly distressed King. [It] was the one instance during the war in which he felt that the President had gone against the advice of his Joint Chiefs of Staff." Walter L. Whitehill, *Fleet Admiral King* (New York: W. W. Norton & Co., 1952), p. 525.

36. Harrison, *Cross-Channel Attack*, p. 38; Matloff and Snell, *Strategic Planning, 1941-1942*, pp, 379–80.

37. Matloff and Snell, *ibid.*, p. 363. Mr. Churchill was delighted and in his response on November 19 used his famous "[soft] underbelly" metaphor, which he had sprung on Stalin at Moscow in October to color the hope of striking into Germany through the Mediterranean. It should be remembered that the ideas embraced in the exchange of messages were part of the basic Anglo-American strategy agreed on at the ARCADIA Conference in December 1941: "In 1943 the way may be clear for a return to the continent across the Mediterranean, from Turkey into the Balkans, or by landings in Western Europe." Sherwood, *Roosevelt and Hopkins*, p. 459.

38. See above, p. 32.

39. The JCS adopted Gen. Handy's proposal to press for "overriding priority for OVERLORD without reservations or conditions" on August 16. Handy then flew to Washington. On the 17th, Roosevelt, who had been entertaining Mr. Churchill at Hyde Park and then gone to Washington, arrived at Quebec. Matloff, *Strategic Planning, 1943-1944*, pp. 220–23.

40. Leighton, "OVERLORD versus the Mediterranean," *Command Decisions*, pp. 255–85; "OVERLORD Revisited"; and letters to the author. Matloff, *ibid.*, pp. 334–67. En route to SEXTANT Marshall said in a conference of the JCS with F.D.R. on the *Iowa*: "if the British insist on going into the Balkans, instead of OVERLORD, we will pull out and go into the Pacific with all our forces." The President parried this by saying that Stalin must be heard on operations up the Adriatic to the Danube. *Ibid.*, pp. 343–44. At Tehran in the first plenary session Mr. Roosevelt did not take up the cudgels for giving OVERLORD overriding priority. On the eve of this session he had told his chiefs that he was "much more favorably inclined toward operations from the Adriatic than from the Dodecanese." *Ibid.*, pp. 359, 360.

41. Matloff and Snell, *Strategic Planning, 1941-1942*, pp. 272–73.

42. Harrison, *Cross-Channel Attack*, pp. 62–63.

43. Matloff and Snell, *Strategic Planning, 1941-1942*, pp. 298ff, especially pp. 303–4. I am assuming that Admiral Leahy was speaking for the President.

44. For Admiral King's requests and the War Department's resistance, *ibid.*, pp. 298–306. For Mr. Roosevelt's position, *ibid.*, p. 379.

45. Henry H. Arnold, *Global Mission* (New York: Harper & Bros., 1949), pp. 355–56.

46. *AAF History*, II, *Europe—*TORCH *to* POINTBLANK, p. 282; Sherwood, *Roosevelt and Hopkins*, p. 623; Leighton and Coakley, *Global Logistics*, p. 396.

47. Emerson, "F.D.R.," p. 164, adopting Matloff's view.

48. Sherwood, *Roosevelt and Hopkins*, p. 603. On May 4, 1942, F.D.R. ordered the War Production Board to raise production requirements for Europe from C to A priority. Matloff and Snell, *Strategic Planning, 1941-1942*, p. 195. When demands for reinforcement of the Pacific, the Middle East, China, and Russia that could be met only at the expense of BOLERO began to mount, in the spring of 1942, Marshall took the issue to the Presi-

dent for decision, on May 6. He replied at once: "I do not want BOLERO slowed down." *Ibid.*, p. 219. TORCH compromised a 1943 ROUNDUP, but Mr. Roosevelt saw it as having saved the "Germany First" strategy. On March 8, 1943, he said to Marshall: "Just between ourselves, if I had not considered the European and African fields in the broadest geographical sense, you and I know that we would not be in Africa today—in fact, we would not have landed in Africa or Europe." Matloff, *Strategic Planning, 1942–1943*, p. 68.

49. "Expanding production capacity had to be directed in accordance with priorities established to fit particular military needs at least a year in advance." Harrison, *Cross-Channel Attack*, p. 33. In a press conference in July, 1943, at the time of the invasion of Sicily, Mr. Roosevelt showed himself well aware of the long back-reach into the nation's productive economy of military requirements for a given campaign. Samuel I. Rosenman, *Working with Roosevelt* (New York: Harper & Bros., 1952), p. 382.

50. F.D.R. had watched war production closely and held a whip hand over it. In his "must" message to Congress on 6 January 1943, he had sternly said: "Let no man say it cannot be done. It must be done and we have undertaken to do it." Smith, *Economic Mobilization*, p. 524. The assumption underlying the Army's "Victory Program" submitted in September, 1941, was that 1 July 1943 would be "the date of the full attainment of U.S. military strength." The final estimate of requirements in that program moved the date when the program could be completed on to the spring of 1944. But the Victory programs had assumed that Russia would not stay in the war, and U.S. production had exceeded all expectations. *Ibid.*, pp. 137–38.

51. Leighton and Coakley, *Global Logistics*, pp. 44, 61.

52. Smith, *Economic Mobilization*, p. 210.

53. At a meeting with Marshall at the White House on 9 August 1943, the President observed that planners are "always conservative" (and that more could be done in the Mediterranean than they thought, without prejudice to OVERLORD). When General Marshall said that the Joint Chiefs would give Mr. Roosevelt's proposals (of further operations in the Mediterranean) a "critical review," Mr. Roosevelt told him that he did not like the word "critical," "since he wanted help in carrying out his idea rather than obstacles placed in the way." Matloff, *Strategic Planning, 1943–1944*, p. 212.

54. According to Admiral Leahy (*I Was There*, p. 103) "planning of major campaigns was always done in close co-operation with the President." In June, 1943, Roosevelt called Leahy, Marshall, and Somervell to a meeting in his bedroom "to express his very strong dissatisfaction with the way our whole show is running in China." Sherwood, *Roosevelt and Hopkins*, p. 739. For Mr. Roosevelt's "system" of control and General Marshall's criticism of its deficiencies, Cline, *Washington Command Post*, pp. 104–6, 312–17. For Field Marshal Sir John Dill's services in keeping Marshall "confidentially" informed of the President's messages to Mr. Churchill, *ibid.*, p. 316.

55. "Roosevelt would adopt ideas only if he agreed with them. If he disagreed, he simply did nothing." Edward Flynn, quoted by Emerson, "F.D.R.," p. 160. For example, at TRIDENT he let ANAKIM die for want of his support. Matloff, *Strategic Planning, 1943–1944*, pp. 141–42.

56. Sherwood, *Roosevelt and Hopkins*, p. 803.

57. "I was a leg man." Leahy, *I Was There*, p. 97. For estimates of Admiral Leahy's value and influence, Emerson, "F.D.R.," p. 159; Ehrman, *Grand Strategy*, VI, p. 341. Professor Ehrman concludes that Leahy was indeed a useful leg man between Mr. Roosevelt and the Joint Chiefs, bringing "a dry if circumscribed intelligence" to bear on their problems, and exercising "a sometimes surprising restraint" on his colleagues.

58. Stimson wrote that he "was often able to present the position of the War Department more effectively through Hopkins than he could in a direct conversation with the President." Stimson and Bundy, *On Active Service*, p. 333.

59. Emerson, "F.D.R.," p. 160.

60. "On 26 October [1942] the President, in a characteristic move, ordered the War Shipping Administration to find 20 additional ships for the South and Southwest Pacific without taking them from either the Soviet aid program or from TORCH." By mid-November WSA had found 64 of the 87 ships the Army and Navy required—"by what magic," the historian adds, "is not clear from the records." Leighton and Coakley, *Global Logistics*, p. 396. In November the President told the JCS and Hopkins that the production of 82,000 combat airplanes in 1943 was a "must." When Leahy and King objected that this would mean delay in essential features of the Navy's program, the President told them "that the aircraft program would not conflict with the Navy program in any way." Sherwood, *Roosevelt and Hopkins*, p. 659. His resolution of the British import tonnage crisis in the spring of 1943 is another example of his refusal to accept "either-or" advice. (Above, p. 62). At Casablanca Hopkins told Churchill that he had come to realize "that the Chiefs of Staff may agree to do nothing today, but tomorrow when the President puts the heat on, they will suddenly decide that they can do a little more than they think they can at this conference." *Ibid.*, p. 688.

61. Leahy, *I Was There*, p. 136.

62. Russia's continuation in the war as a "major factor" is "of cardinal importance" and "must be a basic factor in war strategy." F. D. R. to the Secretary of War, 6 January 1943, Matloff, *Strategic Planning, 1943–1944*, p. 281. When the War Department later in 1943 wanted to make aid to the U.S.S.R. conditional, Roosevelt refused: ". . . in 1943 . . . [it was] White House policy that lend-lease to the U.S.S.R. was not to be used as a basis for bargaining." *Ibid.*, p. 282.

CHAPTER IV

1. *The U.S. Army Air Forces in World War II*, eds. Wesley Frank Craven and James L. Cate, Vols. I–VI (Chicago: University of Chicago Press, 1948–1955)—hereafter cited as *AAF History;* Sir Charles Webster and Noble Frankland, *The Strategic Air Offensive against Germany, 1939–1945*, Vols. I–IV, ed. J. R. M. Butler, United Kingdom Military Series (London: Her Majesty's Stationery Office, 1961, in *History of the Second World War*).

2. The U.S. Strategic Bombing Survey (hereafter cited as USSBS), *Overall Report (European War) Sept. 30, 1945* (Washington, D.C., 1945), p. 38.

3. *AAF History*, VI, *Men and Planes*, p. 7.

4. *Ibid.*, p. 13.

5. Watson, *Chief of Staff*, pp. 278–98; *AAF History*, I, *Plans and Early Operations*, pp. 258–67; Cline, *Washington Command Post*, pp. 23, 67–70; K. R. Greenfield and Robert W. Palmer, "Origins of the Army Ground Forces: G.H.Q., 1940–1942," *Organization of Ground Combat Troops* (Washington, D.C., 1947, in *U.S. Army in World War II*), pp. 134–53.

6. *AAF History*, I, pp. 249–51; VI, p. vii. In August, 1939, the Air Corps had had 800 first-line planes. *Ibid.*, VI, p. 173. At peak strength, in July, 1944, the Army Air Forces had on hand 79,908 planes of all types. *Ibid.*, p. 197. Its strength in personnel expanded from 20,196 in June, 1938 (11 percent of the Army's strength) to 2,372,293 in June, 1944 (31 percent of the Army total). *Ibid.*, p. xxv.

7. *AAF History*, I, pp. 110–12; VI, p. xxv; Robert R. Palmer, "The Procurement of Enlisted Personnel: the Problem of Quality," *Procurement and Training of Ground Combat Troops* (Washington, D.C., 1948, in *U.S. Army in World War II*), pp. 21–28. On 4 August 1942, all aircraft production programs were given AA–1 priority. Smith, *Economic Mobilization*, p. 526.

8. *AAF History*, I, pp. 240, 246–49, 564–65, 607–8, 615–17; Arnold, *Global Mission*, p. 306.

9. *Ibid.*, p. 323; *AAF History*, II, pp. 51ff.

10. *AAF History*, II, pp. 242–58.

11. Churchill, *The Hinge of Fate*, p. 925.

12. Webster and Frankland, II, p. 39.

13. It is generally stated that it was the P–51 ("Mustang") that permitted the Eighth Air Force to resume its raids deep into Germany in February, 1944. William R. Emerson has recently pointed out that it was only in the summer of 1944 that the P–51 "gradually" took over. In the spring the fighter escort used was the P–47 ("Thunderbolt") with droppable belly tanks. Operation POINTBLANK, Harmon Memorial Lecture (Army Air Force Academy, 1962), p. 62.

14. The change of command became effective at midnight 13–14 April. *AAF History*, III, *Europe:* ARGUMENT *to VE Day*, p. 81.

15. *AAF History*, VI, p. 7. Before 7 December 1941, the Army Air Forces had just under 300 heavy bombers. *Ibid.*, p. 204. The Japanese attacks on 7–8 December left the United States with only 631 airplanes suitable for combat.

16. Delivery of B–24's ("Liberators") to the Navy began in August, 1942. By the end of 1944, 964 had been delivered. *AAF History*, I, p. 551n.

17. 107,000 aircraft in all. *AAF History*, II, pp. 291ff. When on 24 August 1942, F.D.R. requested a statement of what was needed for "complete air ascendency over the enemy," the Air War Plans Division on 9 September said that the U.S. would have to produce 139,100 aircraft in 1943. The Navy was flatly opposed. F.D.R. backed the War Department. By 15 October he was ready to declare 131,000 a "must." *AAF History*, II, pp. 288–90.

18. In January, 1943, the Navy, to General Arnold's dismay, requested the diversion of 1,300 shore-based bombers to Navy command by 1 July 1943. He countered with the Air Forces Antisubmarine Command. *AAF History,* I, pp. 538ff.

19. Sir John Slessor, *The Central Blue: Recollections and Reflections* (London: Cassell and Co., 1956), p. 352; Samuel E. Morison, *The Battle of the Atlantic,* in *History of U.S. Naval Operations in World War II,* Vol. I (Boston: Little, Brown & Co., 1947), pp. 115, 245–47.

20. *Ibid.* For B–17's at Midway: Morison, *Coral Sea, Midway, and Submarine Actions,* IV (1949), pp. 110, 150–51, 159n.; *AAF History,* I, pp. 451–62. General Arnold wrote regarding the bad aim of the B–17's in the Midway battle that it was "a thorn in my side for many months." *Global Mission,* p. 379.

21. The AAFAC was activated 15 October 1942. Air Marshal Slessor, Commander-in-Chief of the Coastal Command, found the analogy "imperceptible." Slessor, *Central Blue,* p. 494.

22. *AAF History,* I, pp. 542ff, II, pp. 384–85, 405; Morison, *Battle of the Atlantic,* I, pp. 244–47.

23. *The Memoirs of the General the Lord Ismay* (London: Heinemann, 1960), p. 244. Air Marshal Slessor, who was in Washington on several missions in 1941–43, writes: "The violence of [American] interservice rivalry in those days had to be seen to be believed and was an appreciable handicap to their war effort." Slessor, *ibid.,* p. 494.

24. The Combined Chiefs of Staff originally concurred in the commitment of the 15 groups to the Pacific, in "CCS 94." Matloff and Snell, *Strategic Planning, 1941–1942,* pp. 281, 296. But the first of the 15 groups would not be available for commitment until December, and Marshall backed Arnold in stalling for time, against the pressure of MacArthur and King, throughout August and into September, and in spite of the Guadalcanal crisis. *Ibid.,* p. 301. For Arnold's reasons and his vigorous and stubborn fight, which, late in October he won, see *ibid.,* pp. 321–22; Arnold, *Global Mission,* pp. 321–28, 335, 338.

25. *AAF History,* II, pp. 402ff. A corresponding anxiety and belligerent alarm built up in the Navy: "So many 'boy generals' of the Army Air Forces were propagating the separate air force idea that the Navy feared it would lose its own air arm, and the war." Morison, *Battle of the Atlantic,* I, p. 246.

26. Morison, *The Atlantic Battle Won,* X (1956), p. 28; *AAF History,* II, pp. 392–94.

27. *AAF History,* II, pp. 406–11. For the President's intervention, Matloff, *Strategic Planning, 1943–1944,* p. 49. The Air Forces' historians regard this as a "key decision" regarding "the organization of American military power in World War II." *AAF History,* II, p. 377. See also Morison, *Battle of the Atlantic,* I, pp. 245–46; X, pp. 26–31.

28. General Arnold put combined operations with the ground forces and Navy eighth in his "fundamental" list of priorities for the Army Air Forces. Arnold, *Global Mission,* pp. 290–91.

29. K. R. Greenfield, *Army Ground Forces and the Air-Ground Battle*

Team (Historical Section, Army Ground Forces, Army Ground Forces Studies, No. 35, in lithograph, 1948), pp. 3–5. For the Army Air Forces' case against FM 31–35, *AAF History*, II, pp. 137–45; III, pp. 806–7.

30. Omar N. Bradley, *A Soldier's Story* (New York: Henry Holt & Co., 1951), p. 41.

31. For the rudimentary means of communication between air and ground units in 1943, Greenfield, *Air-Ground Battle Team*, pp. 69–76.

32. *Ibid.*, pp. 9–18, 35–42.

33. "We went into France almost totally untrained in air-ground co-operation." Bradley, *A Soldier's Story*, p. 249. Air-ground co-operation in France became effective "only after a period of intensive combat." General Brereton, quoted in *AAF History*, III, p. 141.

34. For the Army Air Forces' problems in North Africa, *AAF History*, II, pp. 110ff, 132ff.

35. Greenfield, *Air-Ground Battle Team*, pp. 19–20, 45–50.

36. Documentation of the following account of observation aviation for the Army Ground Forces can be found in Chapters III, VI, and IX of the study just cited, which was based on research in the files of Headquarters, Army Ground Forces. In 1946, as the result of an administrative blunder, these important records were largely destroyed.

37. Walter Bedell Smith, *Eisenhower's Six Great Decisions: Europe 1944–45* (New York: Longmans, Green & Co., 1956), p. 144. Of the role of air in stopping the German counterattack at Mortain in August, 1944, Lt. Gen. Bodo Zimmerman, G. 3, *OB West*, has written: "This was the first time in history that an attacking force had been stopped solely by bombing." Seymour Freiden and William Richardson, eds., *The Fatal Decisions*, trans. by Constantine Fitzgibbon (New York: William Sloane Associates, 1956), p. 224.

38. *AAF History*, III, pp. 806–7; Greenfield, *Air-Ground Battle Team*, pp. 47–49.

39. *AAF History*, II, pp. 136–65.

40. Greenfield, *Air-Ground Battle Team*, pp. 76–85; *AAF History*, II, index, s. v. "air-ground co-operation." The devices adopted were suggested by the relations between Montgomery's Eighth Army and the Desert Air Force in their drive across Africa. Montgomery at once publicized these in his *Notes on High Command in War*, which the Air Staff in Washington cited as the justification of FM 100–20. The doctrinal manifesto that proclaimed the separation of American air and ground forces, and the practical measures that brought them together, were inspired by the same source.

41. *AAF History*, III, pp. 134–36.

42. Greenfield, *Air-Ground Battle Team*, pp. 87–92; *AAF History*, III, pp. 196–209. For (1) a summary of the achievements of the Ninth Air Force in the pre-invasion bombing of the French transportation system, *AAF History*, III, pp. 138–81; (2) for the marriage of tactical air commands and armies, *ibid.*, pp. 243–44.

43. *Ibid.*, Martin Blumenson, *Breakout and Pursuit* (Washington, D.C., 1961, in *U.S. Army in World War II*), pp. 333–34; Bradley, *Soldier's Story*, pp. 337–38.

44. *AAF History*, III, p. 808.

45. See note 32. ". . . it was only after a period of intensive combat that air-ground co-ordination reached the remarkable degree of perfection which became so deservedly renowned." Gen. Brereton, Memo for Air Historical Officer, 6 August 1947, cited in *AAF History*, III, p. 141, note 11.

46. *AAF History*, III, pp. 245–46.

47. Greenfield, *Air-Ground Battle Team*, p. 92.

48. Bradley, *Soldier's Story*, p. 337.

49. *AAF History*, IV, *The Pacific—Guadalcanal to Saipan* (1950), and V, MATTERHORN *to Nagasaki* (1953) ; George C. Kenney, *General Kenney Reports* (New York: Duell, Sloane & Pearce, 1949). The Pacific experience is summarized in Greenfield, *Air-Ground Combat Team*, pp. 93–96. See also Jeter Isely and Philip A. Crowl, *The U.S. Marines and Amphibious War: its Theory and Practice* (Princeton: Princeton University Press, 1951).

50. Vice Admiral Robert Ghormley, whose Army Deputy was an Air officer, Maj. Gen. Millard Harmon. General Kenney's Allied Air Forces, in General MacArthur's Southwest Pacific Area, conducted the first attacks on Rabaul. John Miller, jr., CARTWHEEL: *the Reduction of Rabaul* (Washington, D.C., 1959, in *U.S. Army in World War II*), pp. 230–33.

51. In May, 1944. Great Britain, Air Ministry, *The Rise and Fall of the German Air Force, 1933 to 1945* (London: ACAS [I] Pamphlet No. 248, 1948), p. 296.

52. United States Strategic Bombing Survey (hereafter cited as USSBS), *The Effects of Strategic Bombing on the German War Economy*, October 31, 1945 (Washington, D.C., 1945), pp. 11, 139–46, and Exhibit D–1; *Overall Report (European War)*, p. 37; Webster and Frankland, III, pp. 221–23.

53. USSBS, *Effects on German War Economy*, Appendix, Table 102.

54. USSBS, *Overall Report (European War)*, p. 37.

55. *Ibid.*, pp. 37–38.

56. *Ibid.*, p. 95; Webster and Frankland, III, p. 288.

57. In the second half of 1943 the Eighth Air Force was aiming its bombs with increasing accuracy. In July, 12.7 percent, in October, 27.2 percent of its bombs fell within 1,000 feet of the aiming point. The percentage that fell within 2,000 feet rose from 36.7 percent in July, to 53.8 percent in October. *AAF History*, II, p. 697. But even after the B–17's received their fighter escorts, in the spring of 1944, their bombing, which overcast compelled them to do by radar until the "Big Week" of 23 February, was highly inaccurate. *AAF History*, III, p. 52–54. Even in the decisive oil bombing campaign only 3 percent of the bombs dropped by the USSTAF on the three major refineries struck damageable targets. *Ibid.*, p. 795. In 1944, the three strategic air forces vastly increased the combined weight of their attack—in bombers, bombs, and accuracy of aim. Webster and Frankland, III, pp. 3–4. For delivery of bombs of the strategic air forces, by quarters, 1940–45, see USSBS, *Effects on German War Economy*, Tables 1–4, pp. 1–5.

58. *AAF History*, III, p. 787.

59. USSBS, *Effects on German War Economy*, pp. 13–14; *Overall Report* (Europe), p. 38; *Rise and Fall*, pp. 334–36.

60. USSBS, *Effects on German War Economy*, pp. 1ff; Webster and

Frankland, I, *passim.* For the reluctance and step-by-step approach of the British to the bombing of non-military targets, see Butler, *Grand Strategy,* II, pp. 17, 166–71, 182, 409–12, 551–52.

61. For General Eaker's defense of daylight bombing at Casablanca and his hopeful estimate in April, 1943, see *AAF History,* II, pp. 299–304, 366. The Americans "were fanatic about the use of daylight bombing." Webster and Frankland, I, p. 354.

62. Slessor, *Central Blue,* p. 372.

63. Webster and Frankland, I, *passim.* Radio-directed and radar aiming devices ("Oboe" and "H2S") "were not available until early 1943." Slessor, *ibid.,* p. 370. "Pathfinders" were being used earlier. Webster and Frankland, I, p. 249. But by the summer of 1942, the British were on the way to bombing blind "almost as accurately as anyone could bomb visually." Slessor, *ibid.,* p. 429. The British air historians have concluded that "in terms of physical destruction of targets the [U.S.] Eighth Air Force operations had relatively little effect in 1943, especially by comparison with what was being achieved at night by the British." Webster and Frankland, II, p. 4.

64. *AAF History,* III, pp. xiv–xv, 638–39. For a British view of the "moral" issue, Webster and Frankland, II, pp. 22–23.

65. *AAF History,* III, p. 733.

66. Beginning in September, 1943. *AAF History,* II, p. 668.

67. Webster and Frankland, III, pp. 109–10.

68. *AAF History,* III, pp. xvi, 724–25, 737–38, 744. In February, 1944, Spaatz had acquiesced in the bombing of some 30 "towns and villages previously undisturbed" and containing no vital military targets (Operation CLARION). *Ibid.,* p. xvi.

69. *Ibid.,* pp. 725–27, 737–38, 744.

70. *Ibid.,* p. 731.

71. USSBS, *Effects on German War Economy,* p. 1; *AAF History,* III, p. 796; Webster and Frankland, II, pp. 71–72; III, p. 41.

72. USSBS, *Effects on German War Economy,* pp. 5–6.

73. *Ibid.,* p. 13.

74. *AAF History,* V, pp. xviii–xx, 609ff.

75. *Ibid.,* pp. 33ff.

76. *Ibid.,* pp. xviii–xix, 546–76.

77. *Ibid.,* pp. xix–xx; 609–17.

78. But General Arnold knew when he appointed General LeMay to replace General Hansell that LeMay did not believe in selective bombing; and in February he had authorized giving certain "areas" as secondary targets in incendiary attacks and as primary targets "under radar conditions." *Ibid.,* p. 611.

79. *Ibid.,* pp. xx, 615–17. The AAF historians observe that this first attack was "perhaps the most scathing air attack of the whole war." *Ibid.,* p. xx.

80. *Ibid.,* p. 624.

81. *Ibid.,* pp. xx, 754–55.

82. USSBS, *Summary Report (Pacific War),* 1 July 1946 (Washington, D.C., 1946), p. 26. The USSBS reached the same conclusion about Germany. *Overall Report (European War),* p. 38.

83. For the grave risk his ambition to do so led him to take, see *AAF History*, V, pp. 625–27.

84. USSBS, *Summary*, pp. 12–15; *AAF History*, V, pp. xxvi, 739–41.

85. USSBS, *Overall Report (Europe)*, pp. 38, 107.

86. Churchill said, in 1949: "For good, or for ill, air mastery is today the supreme expression of military power, and fleets and armies, however vital and important, must accept a subordinate rank." Speech in Boston, 1949, quoted by Slessor, *Central Blue*, p. xi. It is instructive to compare with this measured statement that which Gen. Karl Koller (Chief of the *Luftwaffe* Operations Staff, September, 1943; Chief of its General Staff, Nov., 1944– May, 1945), made after he had seen the *Luftwaffe* annihilated: "All plans for the defense of a country, a continent, or a sphere of interest or for offensive operations must be in the hands of the Air Force command. The Army and Navy commands are subordinate authorities. Although they cannot be done away with entirely, they must adapt themselves to all requirements in the air, which covers the entire world and extends to high heavens." *Rise and Fall*, p. 409.

INDEX

AAF *History*, I, 127 *n*10; II, 129
*n*46; III, 132 *n*14; IV, 135 *n*49;
V, 135 *n*49; VI, 127 *n*10
Air bombardment. *See* Strategic air
bombardment
Air commands, tactical, 108, 109,
110. *See also* Ninth and Twelfth
Air Forces, XII Air Support
Command, XIX Tactical Air
Command
Air Corps, 87, 88
Air doctrine, 88, 96–97, 101, 104,
108. *See also* Command doc-
trines, air; FM 31–35; FM
100–20
Air forces, German. See *Luftwaffe*
Air forces, U.S., strategic, 91, 93,
103, 110, 112, 118, 121; fighter
escort, 93, 116, 118. *See also*
Eighth, Fifteenth, and Twen-
tieth Air Forces; XXI Bomber
Command; U.S. Strategic Air
Forces, Europe
Air-ground co-operation, 101–12,
121; combat, 101–12; air-tank
team, 110; observation, 101,
104–7; observation, artillery,
105–7; training, 103, 110
Air, naval, 94, 98, 111
Air power, 85–121; decisiveness, 85,
86, 120–21
Air supremacy, 5, 36, 67, 84
Air war, independent, 88, 91, 94, 95,
96, 97, 120, 121
Aircraft production. *See* Production,
military, U.S.
Anti-submarine campaign, 31, 37,
62, 68, 74, 91, 92, 97, 98–100

ANVIL, 34, 40–41
ARCADIA Conference. *See* Conferences, Allied
Armies, U.S. *See* Fifth, First and
Third Armies
Army, U.S., 6, 7, 69, 81, 86, 87, 89,
98
Army Air Forces, 8, 29, 63, 66, 69,
84, 86, 87–122; co-operative strategic missions, 95, 96, 97, 101,
117ff, 120; expansion, 90, 95,
132 *n*6; interservice controversies: with the Navy, 96–100,
107; with the Ground Forces,
97, 100; preferential recruit-
ment, 90
Army Air Forces Antisubmarine
Command, 99, 100
Army Ground Forces, 86, 88, 102,
106
Arnold, Gen. Henry H., 73, 88, 89,
90, 91, 95, 99, 117, 119; *Global
Mission*, 129 *n*45
"Arsenal of Democracy" concept, 74
Atom bomb, 8, 9, 120, 121
Axis, the, 1, 2, 4, 7, 9, 21, 25, 27,
31, 42, 54, 59, 67, 68, 79, 83,
84, 86

Balkans, 17, 33, 42, 70
Blockade, naval, 9, 27; of Japan, 21,
22, 120
Blumenson, *Breakout and Pursuit*,
134 *n*43
BOLERO, 27, 28, 29, 30, 59
BOLERO-ROUNDUP, 27, 28, 29, 32, 57,
73, 79, 91

139